Cognitive Behavioural Therapy for Problem Drinking

This book serves as a concise and practical guide on the application of cognitive behavioural therapy (CBT) to problem drinking. Divided into five chapters it provides:

- a detailed account of the cognitive and behavioural processes involved in the development and maintenance of problem drinking
- in-depth coverage of assessment and case formulation and their role in planning and sequencing CBT interventions
- concise and practical illustrations of the application of CBT interventions in preparing, implementing and maintaining change.

Cognitive Behavioural Therapy for Problem Drinking also includes diaries and worksheets for use with the client making it essential reading for all mental health practitioners in the field of alcohol misuse, as well as a useful resource for those in training.

The appendices of this book contain worksheets that can be downloaded free of charge to purchasers of the print version. Please visit the website www.cbtarena.com/9780415408769 to find out more about this facility.

Marcantonio Spada is Professor of Psychological Therapies at London South Bank University in partnership with North East London NHS Foundation Trust. An expert in cognitive behavioural theory and therapy for problem drinking, he is a practising clinician with extensive experience of working with problem drinkers.

Cognitive Behavioural Therapy for Problem Drinking

A Practitioner's Guide

MARCANTONIO SPADA

Routledge
Taylor & Francis Group

LONDON AND NEW YORK

First published 2010 by Routledge
27 Church Road, Hove, East Sussex BN3 2FA

Simultaneously published in the USA and Canada
by Routledge
270 Madison Avenue, New York, NY 10016

Routledge is an imprint of the Taylor & Francis Group, an Informa business

© 2010 Marcantonio Spada

Typeset in Stone Serif by Garfield Morgan, Swansea, West Glamorgan
Printed and bound in Great Britain by TJ International Ltd, Padstow,
Cornwall
Cover design by Andrew Ward

This publication has been produced with paper manufactured to strict
environmental standards and with pulp derived from sustainable forests.

British Library Cataloguing in Publication Data
A catalogue record for this book is available from the British Library

Library of Congress Cataloging-in-Publication Data
Spada, Marcantonio.
  Cognitive behavioural therapy for problem drinking : a practitioner's
guide / Marcantonio Spada.
       p. cm.
  Includes bibliographical references and index.
 ISBN 978-0-415-40876-9 (pbk.)
  1. Alcoholism—Treatment. 2. Cognitive therapy. I. Title.
  RC565.S64 2010
  616.86'1—dc22

                                                           2010008828

ISBN: 978-0-415-40876-9 (pbk only)

In memory of B.

Contents

Figures and tables

Figures

Tables

About the author

Marcantonio Spada, PhD, is Professor of Psychological Therapies at London South Bank University in partnership with North East London NHS Foundation Trust. An expert in cognitive-behavioural theory and therapy for problem drinking, he has published extensively in academic journals and authored a self-help guide for problem drinking, *Overcoming Problem Drinking*, based on cognitive-behavioural therapy principles. As a practitioner, he has extensive experience of working with problem drinkers, both in community mental health organizations and private practice, and has co-led the development of the Community Alcohol and Drugs Service in Brent, London.

Acknowledgements

This book is the culmination of over ten years' work in the field of cognitive-behavioural therapy for problem drinking. My doctoral research, undertaken at the University of Manchester, addressed the role of metacognitions in problem drinking and was supervised by Professor Adrian Wells, an important mentor. I have also worked with Professor Michael Bruch and Dr Edward Chesser at University College London, where I received training in cognitive-behavioural therapy. This experience played a crucial role in introducing me to the concepts of functional analysis and case formulation in the treatment of complex cases, as problem drinking cases almost always are. With John Doocey, director of the Community Alcohol and Drugs Service based in Brent, London, we were able to design and establish an alcohol and drugs service based on many of the cognitive-behavioural therapy principles outlined in this book. I am grateful to these people and to the many others I have worked with over the years. A special thank you goes to my wife Ana, who has always supported me, and my children, Yasna and Massimo, who provide an endless source of distraction from my work thanks to their play and affection.

Preface

AIMS, SCOPE AND CONCEPTUAL FRAMEWORK

There were two broad aims in writing this book. First, to create a guide for practitioners on cognitive-behavioural therapy (CBT) for problem drinking and second to present a medium-term CBT approach that addresses the more immediate and practical aspects of problem drinking. Alcohol use problems are heterogeneous, ranging in severity and presentation from the heavy-drinking university college student who sporadically misses lectures due to a hangover, to the individual with severe alcohol dependence who experiences serious medical and social consequences of their drinking. Thirty years ago, Thorley (1980) suggested that alcohol problems could be separated into three domains:

1 problems related to acute intoxication (e.g. arrests for drunk driving, fights and accidental injuries)
2 problems related to regular and heavy drinking that often lead to adverse health (e.g. cirrhosis) and psycho-social consequences (psychological difficulties, marital distress, financial problems) and
3 problems related to dependence, including alcohol withdrawal symptoms and longer-term difficulties with work, for example

Whilst the three domains of alcohol problems will often overlap, the majority of people will fall into the second domain: problem drinking. The CBT approach presented in this book is for problem drinking defined as any harmful use of alcohol excluding alcohol dependence (Sobell & Sobell, 1993).

The conceptual framework used in this book is based on developing an understanding of the cause and maintenance of problem drinking and associated problems through the use of the functional analysis and case formulation paradigms. A functional analysis (Cone, 1997) involves building hypotheses regarding the function, or purpose, of target behaviours. Through this tool both client and practitioner can develop a more detailed understanding of the 'mechanics' of behaviour:

⊙ the most frequent and potent antecedents of it
⊙ the short-term positive consequences that serve to maintain it and
⊙ the long-term costs of continuing to engage in it

The central purpose of case formulation is to develop a model, or clinical theory, that can explain how the drinking problem and associated problems developed and are maintained, and consequently how therapeutic interventions should be selected, delivered and sequenced. Case formulation comprises several core elements:

⊙ the description of presenting problems and their exploration through the use of functional analysis
⊙ an integrated developmental profiling
⊙ a problem formulation linking different functional analyses and developmental profiling and
⊙ an explicit plan for therapeutic intervention and sequencing

Adopting a conceptual framework rooted in the functional analysis and case formulation approaches distances somewhat this book from any specific CBT model of problem drinking. The emphasis is therefore on conceptualizing problem drinking issues as ideographically as is possible and allowing for the associated tailoring of therapeutic interventions. This is why this book is termed a 'practitioner's guide' rather than a 'treatment manual'.

WHO IS THIS BOOK WRITTEN FOR?

This book is written for practitioners working in the field of alcohol misuse, who typically come from a range of backgrounds and expertise, including counselling, medicine, nursing, occupational therapy, psychology and social work. It aims to facilitate the development of a theoretical understanding of CBT, but is mainly an aid for clinical practice as it provides a structure of how to work with problem drinking. Though not a prerequisite, basic training in CBT and regular clinical supervision will enhance the usefulness of this book.

This book is descriptive and practical so that those without much CBT experience can use it in everyday practice as an aid when preparing for, or even during, a therapy session. This book will also be of use to practitioners who may be experienced in the delivery of CBT, but have limited exposure to working with problem drinking. Finally, CBT practitioners who have extensive experience in the area of problem drinking will also find this book useful as a companion to practice.

HOW TO USE THIS BOOK

This book, which is divided into five chapters, provides a structured approach for the delivery of therapeutic interventions across the three key areas of CBT for problem drinking (preparing for change, implementing change and maintaining change). It is advisable to move sequentially through these areas; however, therapeutic interventions that fall within these areas can be adapted to the specific needs of the client in terms of sequencing and intensity of their delivery.

Chapter 1 presents an introduction to the theory, principles and therapeutic interventions of CBT and its application to problem drinking. This is particularly important for those who are not familiar with the theoretical underpinnings of CBT. Chapter 2 is aimed at preparing the client for change, and describes assessment procedures, strategies to enhance motivation for change and the principles of case formulation. This chapter also provides a detailed description of key issues in therapy (session structure, time allocation, length of therapy, etc.). Chapter 3 describes fundamental therapeutic interventions targeting the modification of problem drinking, which typically, but not always, are aimed at achieving sobriety. Chapter 4 focuses on therapeutic interventions for maintaining change. Chapter 5 provides information on training and clinical supervision, as well as presenting a case example of CBT for problem drinking.

The cognitive-behavioural therapy approach to problem drinking

INTRODUCTION

The CBT approach to problem drinking is based on the assumption that excessive and harmful alcohol use develops through the interactive processes of classical and operant conditioning, modelling and cognitive mediation (Gorman, 2001). It follows, from this assumption, that contextual and environmental factors are crucial in the initiation, maintenance and change of problem drinking, and that therapeutic interventions should primarily emphasize engagement in new behaviours in contexts that are problematic for the client. A further assumption is that each client presents a unique case that requires a thorough understanding, or a case formulation, in order for CBT to be successful (Spada, 2006a). Approaching each client uniquely entails delineating the particular composition of cognitive-behavioural forces that lead to, and maintain, problem drinking. In addition to adherence to these basic assumptions, CBT for problem drinking places a heavy emphasis on the empirical validity of its models and efficacy of its therapeutic interventions. With these key assumptions as background, let us now turn to considering the processes viewed as central to the initiation, maintenance and change of problem drinking, and to the key therapeutic interventions based on these processes.

BASIC PROCESSES AND THERAPEUTIC INTERVENTIONS

Classical conditioning

Classical conditioning was first investigated, experimentally and systematically, by the Russian physiologist Ivan Pavlov (1928, cited in Mazur, 2002) and has been invoked as the primary process by which environmental (exteroceptive) or internal (interoceptive) cues associated with drinking in the past can come to elicit craving for alcohol in the present.

According to Pavlov's classical conditioning model, a neutral stimulus (NS), such as a blue light, can become rewarding and influence our behaviour because it has reliably preceded a reward (e.g. food). In Pavlov's seminal experiments at the turn of the 20th century, salivation (defined as an unconditioned response; UCR) was demonstrated in dogs presented with food (defined as an unconditioned stimulus; UCS). After a bell (NS) was presented in combination with food (UCS) on a number of occasions, the bell became capable of eliciting salivation (originally an UCR) in the absence of food. Thus the bell had become a conditioned stimulus (CS) and salivation a conditioned response (CR). Diagrammatically presented:

Before conditioning	*During conditioning*	*After conditioning*
Food→salivation	Bell→food→salivation	Bell→salivation
UCS→UCR	NS→UCS→UCR	CS→CR

As an example of classical conditioning applied to problem drinking, consider an individual who drinks in a pub. Alcohol use (UCS) that elicits pleasure (UCR) is paired with a pub (NS) until the pub itself becomes a CS, eliciting a CR. The exact nature of this CR has been debated by many. One possibility is that the response is similar to the withdrawal that occurs when the alcohol that the body has learned to 'expect' is not provided (Ludwig & Wikler, 1974). In other words, exposure to alcohol-related cues would trigger the same responses elicited by withdrawal (such as increased heart rate and salivation). Another hypothesis is that the response is a conditioned compensatory response, that is, a physiological response designed to offset the effects of alcohol (Siegel, 1983). This compensatory process is presumed to facilitate the maintenance of homeostasis in an organism that would otherwise be disturbed by the effects of alcohol. A third possibility (Stewart, Dewit, & Eikelboom, 1984) is that a conditioned appetitive response occurs. This response is similar to that produced by alcohol itself (such as decreased blood pressure), or responses connected with seeking and attaining alcohol (such as arousal to prepare for the activities involved in getting alcohol, and salivation to prepare for ingestion). Evidence suggests that alcohol cues most strongly resemble conditioned appetitive responses (Niaura et al., 1988).

A series of factors will determine whether a CS (e.g. a pub) will elicit a CR (e.g. craving) and include the frequency with which the NS and UCS have been originally paired, the intensity of the CS when it is presented, and the psycho-physiological state of the organism at the time the CS is presented. Classical conditioning theory postulates that problem drinkers actually condition many stimuli in the environment (e.g. paraphernalia) by using alcohol repeatedly, in specific settings, with specific people, and according to specific rituals. The types and varieties of cues that become the CS for alcohol use can therefore be vast, and particular to each individual experience of problem drinking.

Classical conditioning has formed the basis of three prominent therapeutic interventions for problem drinking that will now be briefly reviewed, and also forms part of the theoretical basis for coping skills training (Monti et al., 2002). With the exception of aversion therapies, all these interventions attempt, at least in part, to break the conditioned connection between specific aspects of a drinker's environment and the appetitive responses (craving) presumed to form the motivational basis for alcohol use.

Aversion conditioning

This therapeutic intervention is designed to moderate the reinforcing properties of alcohol by altering the valence of alcohol-related cues (from positive to negative) through counter-conditioning procedures (Howard et al., 1991; Rimmele, Howard, & Hilfrink, 1995). Counter-conditioning entails pairing a CS (like the taste, smell or sight of alcohol) with an aversive stimulus (i.e. one that creates an unpleasant response) so as to condition a new aversive response to both alcohol use and its cues. The conditioning can be accomplished by several means, including apneic paralysis, chemical agents, electric shock or imaginal strategies (also known as covert sensitization). For example, in covert sensitization the image of a drinking situation (e.g. being at a pub) is paired with an imaginal aversive stimulus (e.g. a scene in which the client vomits all over himself or herself).

Stimulus control

This therapeutic intervention is designed to alter environmental cues for drinking by avoiding the cues, rearranging them or implementing different responses in the same environment. For example, avoiding high-risk situations such as going to a pub with friends who are heavy drinkers or walking home from work down a different road so as to avoid specific cues (e.g. a pub).

Cue exposure and response prevention

This therapeutic intervention is designed to extinguish conditioned responses, such as craving, through repeated exposure to the conditioned stimuli (e.g. smell of beer, negative emotion) without the client being able to execute the conditioned response (using alcohol) (O'Brien et al., 1990; Rohsenow et al., 1991).

Operant conditioning

Operant conditioning, or instrumental learning, refers to the way in which the consequences of a behaviour influence the likelihood of that behaviour being repeated (Skinner, 1969; Mazur, 2002). Reinforcement and punishment are the core domains of operant conditioning. These can be either positive (delivered following a response) or negative (withdrawn following a response). This creates a total of four basic consequences: positive and negative reinforcement, and positive and negative punishment.

Positive reinforcement occurs when a response is followed by a favourable stimulus that increases the frequency of a given behaviour. A problem drinker using alcohol (performing an operant response) to attain a feeling of elation is an example of this. Negative reinforcement occurs when a response is followed by the removal of an aversive stimulus thereby increasing the given behaviour's frequency. In the case of a problem drinker, they may use alcohol (perform an operant response) to avoid experiencing craving or to impede withdrawal symptoms. Positive punishment occurs when a response is followed by an aversive stimulus, such as introducing a shock or loud noise, resulting in a decrease of that behaviour. For a problem drinker this may occur if drinking patterns result in punishment such as the suspension of a driving licence following a drink-driving episode. Negative punishment occurs when a response is followed by the removal of a favourable stimulus following an undesired behaviour, resulting in a decrease in that behaviour. For a problem drinker this may occur if drinking patterns result in a partner or spouse withdrawing attention or approval. Extinction occurs when any response that had previously been reinforced is no longer effective.

A wide variety of factors will determine alcohol's capacity to act as a reinforcer. For example, the effectiveness of the consequences of alcohol use will be reduced if the individual's 'appetite' for that source of stimulation has been satisfied. Inversely, the effectiveness of the consequence of alcohol use will increase as the individual becomes deprived of that stimulus. After a response, the immediacy of the felt consequences will determine their effectiveness. More immediate feedback will be more effective than less immediate feedback. If a consequence does not reliably or consistently follow the target response, its effectiveness upon the response will be reduced. However, if a consequence follows the response reliably after successive instances, its ability to modify the response will be increased. Finally, there is a 'cost–benefit' determinant of whether a consequence will be effective. If the size, or amount, of the consequence is large enough to be worth the effort, the consequence will be more effective upon the behaviour. It is important to emphasize that these operant mechanisms function primarily outside conscious awareness.

Operant conditioning has formed the basis of a prominent therapeutic intervention for problem drinking known as contingency management. This intervention is aimed at helping the client re-structure their immediate environments in order to decrease the rewards and increase the costs associated with problem drinking (Higgins, Silverman, & Heil, 2003; Miller, 1975). Strategies typically include:

⊙ providing incentives for compliance with therapy
⊙ positive reinforcement for sobriety (from spouse or friends, for example) and
⊙ negative punishment, in the form of withdrawal of attention and approval, contingent on the resumption of excessive alcohol use

Modelling

Modelling, or vicarious conditioning, involves the observation of another's behaviour and the performance of that behaviour given appropriate reinforcement contingencies (Bandura, 1977). Of the three basic learning processes, modelling is the one that appears to be most efficient and most rapid in producing new learning. According to Bandura (1977), during modelling a process of 'cognitive mapping' occurs in which the individual stores aspects of the behaviour that are later reproduced from this cognitive map. The adequacy of cognitive mapping depends on how well the observer attended to the model's behaviour and the encoding modality (e.g. verbal, visual, tactile, etc.). The more modalities available to encode the behaviour, the more efficiently behaviour is learned.

Whether behaviour learned by observation will actually be performed depends on factors other than cognitive mapping, including the characteristics of the model (e.g. the degree to which the observer holds the model in esteem and as a person to be imitated), whether the model is seen as being reinforced or punished for engaging in the behaviour, whether the observer has an incentive to perform the modelled behaviour and whether the observer expects to be reinforced in a similar fashion to the model if the behaviour is performed.

Modelling processes have been strongly implicated in the development and maintenance of problem drinking. Observing alcohol-using peers may lead to learning and performing these behaviours; furthermore, people will often engage in behaviours that members of their peer group engage in as means of ensuring inclusion in the group.

Modelling provides the theoretical basis for coping skills training (Monti et al., 2002). This therapeutic intervention focuses on training the client to identify high-risk situations for using alcohol, such as negative emotion, craving, social pressure and interactional conflicts. The client is then taught strategies to cope, which include developing drinking refusal skills, problem-solving skills, planning for emergencies, increasing pleasant activities, developing a sober support network, training in assertiveness, effective communication and relaxation.

Cognitive mediation

Human development does not occur on a behavioural level alone. In parallel with the aforementioned learning processes, emotional and cognitive development also takes place. Central to this form of development is language, which is the fundamental tool for the planning of action and for making sense of and giving shape to the environment. According to the cognitive perspective, patterns of action (which may have their root in learning processes) are interpreted and habits of thinking are formed that act as mediators (filters) for other aspects of experience. In this sense, language and inner speech articulate key aspects of experience and also determine our behavioural boundaries: what is thought to be achievable, permissible or possible. From the combination of learning and symbolic experiences, belief systems can emerge that provide frameworks for understanding the self and environment. For example, according to CBT theory an important effect of modelling and/or repeated classical/operant pairings of alcohol with its reinforcing effects is the development of internalized 'expectancies' regarding the effects of alcohol (e.g. Brown, Christiansen, & Goldman, 1987; Christiansen et al., 1989). Expectancies refer to a person's evaluation of an anticipated outcome (Tolman, 1932). In other words, learned information on the association between events. This information is understood to be of an 'if–then' nature; if a certain event is presented, then a certain event is expected to follow. Once acquired, an outcome expectancy is considered to mediate behaviour. Alcohol expectancies are multidimensional, and include both positive and negative effects of alcohol use (Leigh & Stacy, 1993). Positive alcohol expectancies (e.g. "Drinking will make me relax") refer to the drinker's perception of the positive outcomes of drinking, and have been shown to be associated with alcohol consumption (Christiansen et al., 1989; Darkes & Goldman, 1993; Goldman, del Boca, & Darkes, 1999). Negative alcohol expectancies (e.g. "When I drink I have problems driving") refer to the expected negative outcomes that occur as a result of drinking and that have been found, overall, to be less reliably associated with alcohol use (McNally & Palfai, 2001; Stacy, Widaman, & Marlatt, 1990).

Other typologies of cognitive mediators that have been found or hypo-thesized to be responsible for the maintenance of problem drinking behaviour include drinking motives (Cox & Klinger, 1988; Cooper, 1994), permissive beliefs (Beck et al., 1993) and metacognitive beliefs (Spada & Wells, 2006). A belief can be described as a psychological state in which an individual is convinced of the truth of a proposition.

Drinking motives refer to decisional or 'motivational' processes regard-ing alcohol consumption (Cox & Klinger, 1988). They represent the value placed on the particular effects to be achieved through drinking that will motivate a person to drink. Four types of motives have been identified (Cooper, 1994): drinking to obtain social rewards, drinking to enhance positive mood, drinking to deal with negative emotions and drinking to avoid social rejection. Social and enhancement motives have been found to be associated with heavy drinking, with drinking in situations in which heavy drinking is tolerated and with drinking at parties. In contrast, drinking to regulate negative emotions has been found to be associated with solitary drinking, and not with drinking in social situations, such as pubs and bars (Cooper, 1994).

Permissive beliefs (also known as 'rationalizing'; Beck et al., 1993) typically involve themes of entitlement, minimization of aversive conse-quences and justification. Examples include "I deserve a drink" (entitle-ment), "One more won't harm me" (minimization) and "Life is so hard that it does not matter if I drink" (justification). Such beliefs are thought to undermine an individual's ability to tolerate craving. Impaired control beliefs relate to self-perceptions regarding the inability to control drinking ("I cannot control my drinking"). These beliefs are thought to play a central role in lapsing and relapsing.

Metacognitive beliefs refer to the information individuals hold about their internal states and about coping strategies that impact on them (Wells, 2000). General metacognitive beliefs relating to the need to control thoughts (e.g. "I need to control my thoughts at all times") have been found to be associated with and to predict problem drinking (Spada, Caselli, & Wells, 2009; Spada & Wells, 2005; Spada, Zandvoort, & Wells, 2007). Positive metacognitive beliefs about alcohol use relate to the use of alcohol as a means of controlling cognition and emotion (Spada & Wells, 2006, 2008, 2009). Examples may include: "Drinking makes me think more clearly" (problem-solving), "Drinking helps me to control my thoughts" (thought control), "Drinking helps me focus my mind" (attention regulation), "Drinking reduces my self-consciousness" (self-image regulation) and "Drinking reduces my anxious feelings" (emotion regulation). These beliefs are thought to play a key role in the activation of alcohol use as a coping strategy. Negative metacognitive beliefs about alcohol use concern the perception of lack of executive control over alcohol use (e.g. "My drinking persists no matter how I try to control it"), and the evaluation of the negative impact of alcohol use on cognitive functioning (e.g. "Drinking will damage my mind"). These beliefs are thought to play a crucial role in the perpetuation of alcohol use by becoming activated during and following a drinking episode, and triggering negative emotional states that compel a person to drink more (Spada & Wells, 2006, 2008, 2009).

A variety of strategies that fall under the umbrella term 'cognitive therapy' are used to identify, explore and re-structure expectancies and beliefs. These include guided discovery, advantages–disadvantages analysis, thought records, identification of cognitive errors and re-attribution exercises (Beck et al., 1993). Furthermore, behavioural strategies in the form of activity monitoring and scheduling, behavioural experiments, role plays, skills training and relaxation training also serve to test and disconfirm expectancies and beliefs (Beck et al., 1993). Motivational interviewing (Miller, 1983; Miller & Rollnick, 2002), which is a therapeutic intervention developed specifically to work with ambivalence about alcohol use, also focuses on cognitive dimensions of functioning. It targets building the client's motivation and commitment to change through a variety of predominantly cognitive strategies, such as expressing empathy, recognizing discrepancies between goals and current behavioural patterns, and exploring the consequences of actions.

The development and maintenance of problem drinking

The CBT approach views the initiation of alcohol use as primarily due to a combination of environmental factors (such as the availability of alcohol, and parental and peer-group attitudes) and idiosyncratic physiological responses to initial use, resulting in alcohol being either reinforcing or punishing for the individual. The combined effect of these factors in the development of alcohol use will typically lead to the formation of expectancies regarding the reinforcing properties of alcohol. These appear to play an important role in both the continuation and escalation of early drinking behaviour.

With increased use the individual begins to recognize the role that alcohol plays in reducing negative emotion/increasing positive affect and may gradually fail to learn (especially if this happens earlier in life) alternative coping responses to deal with life stressors. Some individuals may, by virtue of personality factors (e.g. impulsivity and sensation-seeking), use alcohol initially for its excitement-producing properties rather than as a maladaptive coping response.

The processes presumed to operate in the development of problem drinking at the less severe stages are largely modelling, operant conditioning and cognitive mediation. With repeated alcohol use, and a move into dependence, classical conditioning processes (conditioned craving and withdrawal) will begin to emerge. At severe levels of dependence, alcohol use will often be exclusively driven by the reinforcing value of avoiding withdrawal (negative reinforcement) rather than the pleasurable effects of using.

At this stage, as alcohol use begins to assume a greater role in the individual's life, the negative consequences of using (e.g. family, health, work or legal problems) will also increase dramatically. This may result in a further increase in alcohol use in an effort to cope with negative emotions arising as a consequence of these problems. As the severity of an individual's predicament escalates, stereotyping and use limited to specific environments will emerge. These settings and the associated stimuli may then become powerful psycho-physiological triggers prompting even greater use.

Although the nature and typology of reinforcement for alcohol use may change over the course of an individual's problem drinking history, principles of classical conditioning, operant conditioning, modelling and cognitive mediation are believed to underpin it. In the many documented cases in which problem drinkers stop using alcohol on their own without any therapeutic intervention, a combination of shifting reinforcement contingencies and cognitive changes appear to explain the modification in behaviour (Sobell & Sobell, 1993).

EMPRICAL RESEARCH ON THEORY AND THERAPEUTIC INTERVENTIONS

The empirical validation of CBT has been an integral part of its philosophy from the beginnings of the behaviour therapy movement in the early 1950s. Not only are CBT theories and therapeutic interventions open to scientific scrutiny, they insist on it. Without well-designed experimental studies of therapy outcomes, CBT theorists and practitioners believe that little or no progress can be made toward resolving the most difficult issue when treating problem drinking: what works best under which conditions and with which client. A recent review of the effectiveness of therapy for problem drinking reported that CBT interventions offer the best chance of success at a reasonable cost (Raistrick, Heather, & Godfrey, 2006). In the 'Mesa Grande' study, a large systematic analysis of problem drinking therapy outcome research (Miller, Wilbourne, & Hettema, 2003), 381 randomized controlled therapy trials were reviewed. For each therapy modality, scores weighted for methodological quality and outcome evidence were summed across studies. This produced a cumulative evidence score (CES), by which the 48 therapy modules included in the review could be ranked. Many of the therapy modalities that had the highest positive scores (therefore a strong evidence supporting the approach) were psycho-social therapeutic interventions rooted in CBT theory and practice. These included, in order of rank, brief interventions, motivational enhancement, community reinforcement, self-change manuals, behavioural self-control training, behaviour contracting (contingency management), social skills training, behavioural marital therapy, aversion therapy and cognitive therapy.

CONCEPTUAL FRAMEWORKS

A variety of CBT conceptual frameworks addressing the causes, maintenance and therapy of problem drinking have been developed. While they do not all focus on exactly the same cognitive-behavioural elements, there is a fair degree of overlap between them, and sometimes different words are used to describe very similar concepts. This section includes a brief description of the three most important conceptual frameworks, followed by a description of the conceptual framework that will be adopted in this book.

The relapse prevention model

The most influential relapse prevention theory, by Marlatt and Gordon (1985), puts forward both a conceptual framework of relapse and a set of therapeutic interventions to curtail or limit relapse episodes. The model (see Figure 1.1) views relapse as a two-stage process. Initial use of alcohol following abstinence is termed a lapse. This arises from a variety of sources including:

⊙ exposure to a high-risk situation
⊙ the lack of availability and/or use of coping skills to handle the high-risk situation without resorting to alcohol use
⊙ poor levels of self-efficacy expectancies to deal with the situation without needing to consume alcohol and
⊙ expectancies that alcohol use will offer an effective means to cope with the situation

A lapse may escalate to further and extensive alcohol use (relapse) primarily as a result of the views an individual holds about a lapse. If the lapse is attributed to negative personal, global and enduring qualities, it is more likely to escalate into a relapse. A typical example of such an attribution is "I do not have enough willpower to stop drinking". The cognitions (and associated negative emotion) hypothesized to follow from a lapse are described as the 'abstinence violation effect' (AVE; Marlatt & Gordon, 1985). However, if an individual views the lapse as a minor mistake and learning opportunity, then he or she is more likely to return to a pre-lapse therapy goal.

A central aspect of the relapse prevention model is the linear progression of responses in high-risk situations. A variety of situations can play a role in relapse episodes (Marlatt & Gordon, 1985; Witkiewitz, Marlatt, & Walker, 2005), including:

⊙ negative and positive emotional states
⊙ social pressure
⊙ exposure to alcohol-related stimuli or cues and
⊙ non-specific cravings

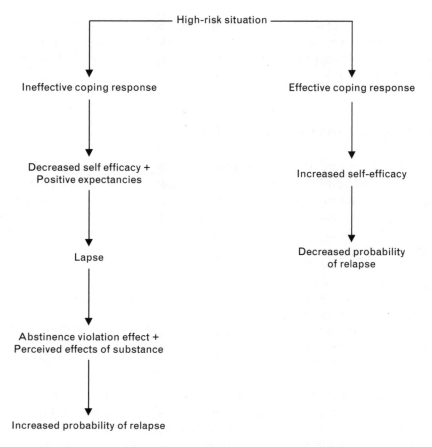

Figure 1.1 The cognitive-behavioural model of the relapse process (Marlatt & Gordon, 1985)

Although the relapse prevention model considers high-risk situations as the immediate relapse trigger, it is actually the individual's response to the situation that will determine whether he or she will experience a relapse. Thus, an individual who can execute effective coping responses (e.g. a cognitive strategy such as positive self-talk or a behavioural strategy such as leaving the situation) will decrease the chances of relapse compared with a person lacking these skills. In addition, people who have managed to cope successfully with high-risk situations will experience a heightened sense of self-efficacy (Bandura, 1977; Marlatt & Gordon, 1985). However, if ineffective coping responses are implemented, then self-efficacy will decline and positive expectancies will become more salient, leading to an increased likelihood of a relapse occurring.

The cornerstone of relapse prevention therapy is the identification and modification of deficits in coping skills, the bolstering of self-efficacy, the challenging of positive expectancies and education on the abstinence violation effect (Witkiewitz et al., 2005).

The coping skills training model

This model, which builds on Marlatt and Gordon's work, was developed by Monti and colleagues (1995). The emphasis is, as its name suggests, on educating/training the client in how to revise skills or develop and use new ones in their life. Why? Because acquiring new skills reduces the risk of relapse by increasing self-efficacy. Coping skills training thus involves the client identifying high-risk situations for using alcohol, such as negative emotional states, urges/cravings, social pressure and experiencing interpersonal conflicts. The client is then taught behavioural strategies to cope, which include developing drink refusal skills, problem-solving skills, planning for emergencies, increasing pleasant activities, developing a sober support network, training in assertiveness, effective communication and relaxation (Monti et al., 2002).

The cognitive model

Schema theory (Beck, 1976) is based on the idea that mental health problems are linked with a disturbance in thinking. Specifically, mental health problems are precipitated by the activation of dysfunctional schemas. Schemas are memory structures that contain two types of information: beliefs and assumptions. Beliefs are key (or 'core') constructs that are unconditional (e.g. "I'm unlovable"; "the world is a dangerous place") and are acknowledged as truths about the self and the world. Assumptions, on the other hand, are conditional and denote contingencies between events and appraisals (e.g. "If I fail an exam it means I must be stupid"). The dysfunctional schemas that are characteristic of mental health problems are considered to be rigid, inflexible and concrete, and schema content is thought to be specific to the given problem (Beck, 1976). Once activated (by external events, drugs or endocrine factors; Beck, 2005), dysfunctional schemas initiate biases in the processing and interpretation of information, systematically distorting the individual's construction of his or her experiences, leading to a variety of cognitive errors (e.g. abstraction, personalization, overgeneralization; Beck, 2005).

These biases are manifested at a surface level as negative automatic thoughts (NATs) in the stream of consciousness. These thoughts form the content of a specific mental health problem.

Beck and colleagues (1993) suggest that at the core of problem drinking is a set of addictive beliefs that are derived from dysfunctional core beliefs. These dysfunctional core beliefs interact with life stressors to produce unpleasant affect (e.g. anxiety, stress; Beck et al., 1993). In turn, unpleasant affect activates alcohol-related beliefs and craving. Individuals who hold beliefs that they cannot tolerate unpleasant affect will tend to be hyper attentive to it and build expectations (permissive beliefs) that it can be relieved through drinking.

In the complete schema model of alcohol abuse (see Figure 1.2), high-risk stimuli (that may be both internal and external) are presented as its first step. External stimuli serve as cues for alcohol use: for example, seeing a pub or a drinking pal. Internal stimuli are emotional or physiological states that remind individuals of times they used in the past and/or arouse a desire to use. These high-risk stimuli trigger alcohol-related beliefs. The latter are dysfunctional viewpoints about alcohol and its use. They typically include beliefs about the positive effects of alcohol use on unpleasant affect. Automatic thoughts are instantaneous ideas and images that intrude in the individual's consciousness when alcohol beliefs are activated. Such thoughts will often involve stereotypic exclamations such as "Go for it!" or "One more time!" These thoughts assist in increasing craving and drive an individual toward using alcohol. Permissive beliefs (also known as 'rationalizing'; Beck et al., 1993) involve themes of entitlement, minimization of aversive consequences and justification of alcohol use. These beliefs lead to the initiation of spurious arguments aimed at tipping the decision-making scale toward alcohol use. Instrumental strategies are the behavioural steps that individuals take to attain and use alcohol. Examples include going to a bar and borrowing money. Finally using alcohol occurs. Although this represents the seventh and final component in the model, it is not an 'outcome' per se, as prolonged alcohol use fuels the development of unpleasant affect, which in turn leads to more alcohol use.

Cognitive therapy is highly active, directive, structured and geared towards the client's acquisition of psychological skills in a time-effective manner (Beck et al., 1993). When applied to problem drinking, cognitive therapy focuses on three main areas in order to help the client toward the ideal goal of abstinence (Beck et al., 1993):

1 modifying maladaptive beliefs about alcohol-related behaviours
2 teaching important life skills and

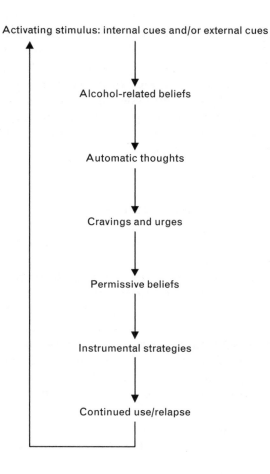

Figure 1.2 The schema model of alcohol abuse (Beck et al., 1993)

3 changing views about the self, the present and the future (the 'cognitive triad'; Beck, 1976)

A variety of strategies are used to restructure maladaptive beliefs, including:

⊙ guided discovery
⊙ advantages–disadvantages analysis
⊙ downward arrow strategy (in this technique the meaning of a thought is repeatedly questioned in order to arrive at assumptions and core beliefs) and
⊙ daily thought records (Beck et al., 1993)

Behavioural strategies in the form of activity monitoring and scheduling, behavioural experiments, role plays, skills training and relaxation training are used to disconfirm beliefs (Beck et al., 1993). From this perspective it is also crucial to tackle comorbid mental health problems. For instance, since anxiety and depression are often a cue for drinking, the above-mentioned interventions may go hand in hand with classical cognitive therapeutic interventions for these mental health problems (Beck, Emery, & Greenberg, 1985).

Proposed conceptual framework

CBT as presented in this book is a medium-term focused therapy, which addresses some of the more immediate and practical aspects of problem drinking and associated problems. The conceptual framework used in this book is based on developing an understanding of the cause and maintenance of a given drinking behaviour and associated problems through the use of functional analysis. Functional analysis (Cone, 1997) involves building hypotheses regarding the function, or purpose, of target behaviours. This involves observing and measuring behaviours and their consequences. Through this tool both client and practitioner can develop a detailed understanding of the 'mechanics' of any behaviour:

- the most frequent and potent antecedents of it
- the short-term positive consequences that serve to maintain it and
- the long-term costs of continuing it

The reality of clinical practice usually entails the identification of multiple problems as targets of therapy. An individual presenting with problem drinking will typically display a variety of associated problems. This complicates clinical pictures with regard to the choice and sequencing of therapeutic interventions. Often, when faced with a drinking problem, practitioners choose to focus on this to the detriment of associated problems, or address all problems concurrently. Both these approaches may work, especially if the presented problems are few in number. However, if the clinical picture is complex, a third option may be needed so as to increase the likelihood of selecting and sequencing the appropriate therapeutic interventions and maximizing the chance of a positive outcome. This option entails delineating in detail the particular composition of cognitive-behavioural forces that have led to and maintain the totality of problems presented: in other words, developing a case formulation. A case formulation will contain several core elements:

⊙ a description of presenting problems
⊙ developmental profiling
⊙ integration of functional analyses and
⊙ explicit guides for intervention modalities and sequencing

The case formulation protocol presented in this book is adapted from the University College London (UCL) case formulation paradigm (Bruch & Bond, 1998).

Both the functional analysis framework and the case formulation approach will be illustrated and discussed in greater detail in the following chapter.

Preparing for change

ASSESSMENT

Introduction

Once the client has agreed to enter therapy, a thorough assessment needs to be undertaken. The central aim of this phase is to evaluate the severity of the drinking problem presented. A client suffering from high levels of alcohol dependence, which interferes with normal functioning, may be unsuitable for CBT and may have to be referred for other therapy (i.e. detoxification). Indeed, researchers have found that errors in estimating alcohol dependence may be a problem in therapy and practitioners ought to be aware of such hazard (Babor, del Boca, & McRee, 1997).

The process of assessing a drinking problem can be segmented into four stages: screening, determination of severity, determination of impact, and determination of motivation and relapse. The first stage begins with screening. The basic question is whether a drinking problem is present, and whether further assessment is required. If screening alerts to the presence of a drinking problem, further assessment is needed to determine its severity. The second stage involves using a variety of modalities (e.g. standardized psychometric instruments, medical examinations, physiological measures or a combination thereof) to attain a full description of the extent and nature of the drinking problem experienced. The third stage focuses on evaluating the impact of the drinking problem on the client's daily life so that appropriate therapeutic interventions can begin to be formulated. The fourth and final stage involves determining whether and why the client would consider it desirable to change his or her lifestyle and pattern of drinking behaviour. The success of any therapy, and the probability of relapse, will depend to a large extent on motivational determinants. Hence, such factors call for careful assessment.

Before looking at each assessment phase in greater detail, it is important to consider factors that can affect the assessment process and the validity of the data it yields. Among other factors are the presence of others during assessment (e.g. a spouse), the consequences for the client of the information revealed, beliefs about the client held by the practitioner (e.g.

that the client will never be able to change) and the client's motivation to stop drinking. The validity of the data obtained in the assessment will also be improved by ensuring the client is sober during the assessment and is not experiencing withdrawal. It is imperative to clearly and openly explain the purpose of assessment and ensure that the client provides information without coercion. Confidentiality needs to be clearly high-lighted and discussed, and feedback during the course of the assessment has to be given in a non-judgemental fashion.

Screening

This initial phase of assessment is aimed at determining the presence of a drinking problem. A variety of instruments based on self-report or objec-tive data are available. The following is a selection of these instruments.

Self-report data

Alcohol Use Disorders Identification Test (AUDIT; Babor et al., 1992)
The AUDIT was developed as a simple screening tool by the World Health Organization (WHO) for early identification of problem drinkers. It consists of 10 questions regarding recent alcohol consumption, alcohol-related problems and alcohol dependence symptoms. Answers are given on a 0–4 rating scale and a total score of 5 is considered the lowest acceptable cut-off point for problem drinking. A total score of 20 or above is considered a cut-off point for severe alcohol dependence. This instru-ment has been extensively used and possesses good validity and reliability.

CAGE (Mayfield, McLeod, & Hall, 1974)
CAGE comprises four questions designed to identify problem drinkers:

1 Have you ever felt you needed to Cut down on your drinking?
2 Have people Annoyed you by criticizing your drinking?
3 Have you ever felt Guilty about your drinking?
4 Have you ever felt you needed a drink first thing in the morning (Eye-opener) to steady your nerves or to get rid of a hangover?

One or more "yes" response constitutes a positive screening test. This instrument has been extensively validated for use in identifying problem drinking.

TWEAK (Russell et al., 1994)

TWEAK is a modification of the CAGE and was originally developed to screen for risk during pregnancy. It can also be used to screen for problem drinking in the general population. The instrument comprises five questions:

1 **T**olerance: (a) How many drinks can you hold; or (b) How many drinks does it take before you begin to feel the first effects of the alcohol?
2 **W**orried: Have close friends or relatives worried or complained about your drinking in the past year?
3 **E**ye openers: Do you sometimes take a drink in the morning when you first get up?
4 **A**mnesia: Has a friend or family member ever told you about things you said or did while you were drinking that you could not remember?
5 **K**ut down: Do you sometimes feel the need to cut down on your drinking?

A 7-point scale is used to score the test. The Tolerance question scores 2 points if (a) the client reports he or she can hold more than five drinks without falling asleep or passing out, or (b) if it is reported that three or more drinks are needed to feel high. A positive response to the Worry question scores 2 points. Positive responses to the last three questions score 1 point each. A total score of 3 or 4 usually indicates harmful drinking. In an obstetric client, a total score of 2 or more indicates the likelihood of harmful drinking.

Objective data

For recent alcohol use (up to 2 days), the breathalyser test gives a quantitative reading of blood alcohol content (BAC) levels, the dipstick in saliva test gives qualitative measurements of alcohol use as does the sweat patch. These readings will be directly affected by the client's weight and the length of time elapsed since the most recent drinking episode.

For the screening of alcohol use for up to several weeks, an effective test is the carbohydrate deficient transferring (CDT) test (Conigrave et al., 2002). After drinking for at least a week (5–8 drinks a day), elevations become noticeable. These remain for at least 20 days post consumption.

Physical markers of chronic alcohol use typically include having a red face and spider nevi which are lower abdomen blood-engorged moles with tiny projections. Liver function tests can also provide good indicators of liver damage after chronic abuse of alcohol. Enzyme assays such as alanine aminotransferase (AST), alkaline phosphatase (APP), aspartate aminotransferase (AST) and gamma glutamyl transaminase (GGT) are used as markers.

Determination of severity

If the screening result suggests a potential drinking problem, further assessment is necessary to determine its severity. Typically, standardized instruments (particularly those that are brief and less structured) are administered. A formal diagnostic interview may be more appropriate in specialized treatment settings, while shorter questionnaires may be warranted in community or primary health centres. When the client appears unwell, there is usually reason to suspect the effects of alcohol dependence. A number of signs typically suggest that the client may be physically dependent on alcohol. These include daily drinking, drinking regularly and intermittently throughout the day, and morning drinking. If a client reports awakening with fears, trembling or nausea, these are also suggestive of dependence. Furthermore, cessation or substantial decrease in drinking will result in the appearance of minor withdrawal symptoms such as tremulousness, nausea, vomiting, irritability and temperature. Such symptoms usually begin within 5–12 hours. More severe withdrawal symptoms (such as seizures, delirium or hallucinations) may also occur, usually within 24–72 hours of the cessation of drinking. Therefore, making several determinations is necessary in order to assess whether the symptoms presented are a signal of withdrawal. In general, the presenting symptoms will reflect the acute effects of intoxication.

A medical history and examination should accompany routine screening for problem drinking, be undertaken when the screening indicates that a drinking problem is likely to exist, or be incorporated into an all-inclusive assessment of a client identified as having a drinking problem. The following is a short list of adverse physical consequences that should be monitored (with the understanding that the practitioner will have to engage the help of a medical doctor to do so):

⊙ cardiac (enlarged heart), endocrine (gynecomastia), gastrointestinal (gastritis) and hepatic (cirrhosis, hepatitis) problems
⊙ immune system impairment
⊙ pancreatitis and
⊙ sleep disorders

In collaboration with the medical doctor, the CBT practitioner may use a variety of self-report instruments. These would typically include:

Alcohol Dependence Scale (ADS; Skinner & Allen, 1982)
The ADS provides a quantitative measure of the severity of alcohol dependence. It consists of 25 questions that assess withdrawal symptoms,

impaired control over drinking, awareness of a compulsion to drink, increased tolerance to alcohol and salience of drink-seeking behaviour. Instructions can be altered for use as an outcome measure at 6, 12 and 24 months. Cut-off points of 14, 22 and 31 indicate moderate, substantial and severe levels of alcohol dependence, respectively. The ADS has been found to possess good validity and reliability.

Clinical Institute Withdrawal Assessment for Alcohol revised (CIWA-Ar; Sullivan et al., 1989)
The CIWA-Ar is a 10-item scale for the clinical quantification of the severity of alcohol withdrawal that evaluates the following:

⊙ autonomic reactivity such as pulse rate and perspiration
⊙ anxiety, agitation, tremors, nausea or vomiting, headache and
⊙ transient tactile, auditory or visual disturbances

A score of 15 or above is considered a cut-off point for increased risk of severe alcohol withdrawal effects such as confusion or seizures. As with the other scales presented, the CIWA-Ar has been found to be valid and reliable.

Determination of impact

In this phase of the assessment, the impact of the drinking problem on the client's daily life is evaluated. This is necessary for two reasons:

1 to inform the case formulation and therefore determine appropriate therapeutic interventions and
2 to note ongoing progress or relapse

Areas covered by this part of the assessment include drinking behaviour, psychological state, interpersonal stressors and neuropsychological impact.

Drinking behaviour

In addition to quantity and frequency of alcohol use, it is important to obtain a clear and detailed description of the drinking style (i.e. continuous vs binge), typical drinking situations and antecedents of drinking, and knowledge about the duration of the individual's drinking problem and previous attempts to stop drinking. Three types of self-report data can be used in order to assess alcohol consumption currently and retrospectively.

Quantity Frequency Scale (QFS; Cahalan, Cisin, & Crossley, 1969)

The QFS is a measure of alcohol consumption levels, with items assessing the dimensions of quantity and frequency of alcohol beverages consumed over a period of 30 days. This measure consists of three questions ("Have you been drinking any beer/wine/spirits over the last 30 days?"; "About how often do you consume beer/wine/spirits?" and "About how much beer/wine/spirits do you drink on a typical day when you drink beer/wine/spirits?"). These are repeated for each of the major alcohol beverage categories (beer, wine and distilled spirits). The total scores from the different alcohol beverage categories are then added together and an estimated daily (or weekly) level of alcohol consumption can be computed. This instrument has been extensively used and possesses good validity and reliability.

Timeline Follow Back Interview (Sobell et al., 1996)

The TLFB is a structured interview tracking 12 calendar months leading up to the assessment. It can also be administered via telephone or computer. The aim of this assessment method is to obtain estimates of daily drinking by asking the client to provide retrospective estimates of their daily drinking over a specified time period. A variety of memory aids can be used to enhance recall (e.g. calendar, key dates). This interview can generate a wide range of data about drinking behaviour (e.g. pattern, variability and magnitude) as well as related problems and their relationship to problem drinking. The TLFB has been shown to have good psychometric properties.

Self-Monitoring or Record Keeping (Sobell & Sobell, 1993)

This assessment strategy involves the client recording the occurrences of alcohol use as well as the conditions that precede, accompany, and follow it. The client is requested to keep a drinking diary (see Table 2.1 for an example) of the number and types of drinks consumed and the particular situations and times when drinking occurred.

This assessment strategy has the advantage, over other strategies, of being independent from retrospective self-reporting. Self-monitoring is especially useful for assessing alcohol consumption and problems after therapy initiation and during follow-up because:

Table 2.1 Drinking diary

Week: 02/08/03	Morning	Units	Afternoon	Units	Evening	Units	Total units
Mon			Pub with friends	4	At home alone, watching a movie	6	10
Tue							
Wed					Dinner with work colleagues	6	6
Thu			Pub alone	4	Alone at home sitting around doing little	2	6
Fri			Pub alone	4		4	4
Sat			Pub with friends	5	Dinner with Annette	5	10
Sun	Lunch with Marcus and Francesca	4					4

⊙ it provides a relatively objective and continuous record with which to evaluate progress and setbacks and
⊙ it demands the client play an active role in the assessment process, enhancing motivation to reduce or quit drinking by raising self-awareness

The downside of this typology of assessment tool is that consistent record keeping may be problematic, particularly among chronic problem drinkers who may lack motivation, organizational skills and social support. It is crucial for the practitioner to decide the level of confidence they have in the client's capability of reporting behaviour accurately and honestly.

Mental health state

Mental health problems are closely associated with problem drinking. This is why the practitioner needs to obtain some preliminary information about the client's mental health state, particularly in the areas of anxiety and mood disorders. In later phases (case formulation), mental health problems can be investigated in more detail. Some of the most commonly used instruments offer indices of trait- and state-dependent affect and include:

⊙ the Symptom Checklist 90 (SCL-90; Derogatis, 1977), which assesses the domains of depression, distress, hostility, interpersonal sensitivity, obsessive-compulsive features, paranoid ideation and psychoticism
⊙ the Beck Anxiety Inventory (BAI; Beck et al., 1988), which measures anxiety
⊙ the Beck Depression Inventory (BDI; Beck et al., 1961), which measures depression and
⊙ the Spielberger State-Trait Anger Inventory (STAXI; Spielberger, Russell, & Crane, 1983), which is a good measure for anger expression and anger control

Interpersonal stressors

The practitioner may also benefit from assessing the type and severity of interpersonal stressors in the client's immediate and familial environment. This is because motivation and success can depend heavily on the early identification and amelioration of such difficulties. A number of assessment tools can be used for this purpose, including:

⊙ the Dyadic Adjustment Scale (Spanier, 1976, 1979), which includes 40 questions that comprise four subscales (affect expression, cohesion, consensus and satisfaction)
⊙ the Life Stressors and Social Resources Inventory (LISRES; Moos et al., 1988), which includes 16 scales related to life and social stressors and

⊙ the Family Environment Scale (FES; Moos, 1990), which evaluates three familial domains (personal growth, relationship and system maintenance) in a 90-True/False questions format

Neuropsychological impact

The most commonly used instrument for screening cognitive function is the Mini Mental State Examination (MMSE; Folstein, Folstein, & McHugh, 1975). This examination can be used to indicate the presence of cognitive impairment and is more sensitive than using informal questioning or an overall impression of the client's orientation. The instrument is limited, however, because it will not detect subtle impairment. Scores of 25–30 are considered normal; 18–24 indicate mild to moderate impairment; and 17 or less severe impairment. For a more formal and in-depth assessment of the impact of alcohol use on neurocognitive processes, the Wisconsin Card Sorting Test (WCST; Heaton et al., 1993) and certain subtests of the Wechsler Adult Intelligence Scale (WAIS; Wechsler, 1997), such as block design, digit-symbol, coding and Trails B, can be used.

Determination of motivation and risk of relapse

The consideration of the problem drinker's motivation for change is paramount in therapy. The practitioner must be aware of whether and why the client would consider it desirable to change their pattern of alcohol use. Involved are issues related to the client's awareness of the impact of problem drinking on their life, and of self-mastery and barriers to successful therapeutic outcomes. Not surprisingly, the success of therapy and the probability of relapse depend, in large part, on motivational determinants. Hence, such factors require a careful assessment.

Motivation

The practitioner must become aware of:

⊙ whether and why the client wants to change his/her lifestyle and pattern of alcohol use
⊙ the client's drinking and other therapy goals
⊙ the client's stage of change and
⊙ the degree to which the client perceives negative consequences of their current drinking pattern and potential consequences of change

Two key measures can be used to assess the stage of change of the client and expectancies about alcohol use respectively:

Stages of Change and Therapy Eagerness Scale (SOCRATES; Miller & Tonigan, 1996)
This instrument assesses recognition, ambivalence and taking steps relative to the client's problem.

Alcohol Expectancy Questionnaire (AEQ; Brown et al., 1980)
This instrument assesses the client's reasons for drinking, primarily phrased in terms of expected positive effects obtained by drinking. A version for adolescents is also available.

Evaluating the risk of relapse

To get a good understanding of what moved the client to consume alcohol in the first place and to relapse after they had decided to abstain or engage in controlled drinking, a number of assessment tools are useful, including:

Reasons for Drinking Questionnaire (RDQ; Zywiak et al., 1996)
This instrument assesses the reasons for alcohol use after a period of abstinence.

Coping Behaviors Inventory (CBI; Litman et al., 1983)
This instrument consists of 36 questions that assess how the client copes with his or her drinking habits.

Corroboration of data

The reliability of an individual's self-report of alcohol use and related problems remains an issue of debate. The balance of the scientific literature suggests that problem drinkers' self-reporting is relatively accurate, and can be utilized with a degree of confidence (Sobell & Sobell, 1993). However, in light of the concerns about the reliability of client self-reports, practitioners may benefit from exploring collateral sources to gather further assessment data. These may include the client's friends, spouses or employers. It is important to note that even with these sources reliability remains questionable. For example, the client's friends with whom they drink may have ample information about drinking habits, but may be difficult to locate for purposes of interviewing or may be unwilling to divulge the information. Spouses may spend much time with the client but often do not know what he or she does in secrecy. Employers may know much about the impact alcohol use has on a client's performance but not about specific drinking patterns. In general, while discrepancies in obtained information are difficult to reconcile, the practitioner cannot assume that the client is untruthful. Instead, minimizing the factors that may lead to biased information is paramount.

Selection of assessment components

Practitioners may wish to combine different assessment tools. Collecting assessment information from multiple modalities will enhance the degree of confidence that practitioners have in the client's self-reports regarding alcohol use and in the overall characterization of the drinking problem. However, this will have to be balanced with the risk of over-burdening (over-assessing) the client during the particularly sensitive period at the beginning of therapy. Ultimately, the selection of the components of a comprehensive clinical assessment will be at the discretion of the practitioner, as will the intensity of its delivery.

Structured interviews

Finally, there are practitioners who prefer to use comprehensive structured or semi-structured interviews to assess their client's drinking problem. A sample of such instruments are as follows: The Alcohol Use Inventory (AUI; Wanberg, Horn, & Foster, 1977) comprises 147 questions about a variety of areas related to problem drinking (for example, motivation for drinking, physical dependence, readiness for change, styles of drinking). More comprehensive versions of the AUI are available (Horn, Wanberg, & Foster, 1990). The Addiction Severity Index (ASI; McLellan et al., 1992) provides data about the client's drug and alcohol use, including problems in employment, family relationships, legal predicament, psychiatric status, and more. The Comprehensive Drinker Profile (CDP; Miller & Marlatt, 1984) is used to identify problem drinking and associated situations, behaviours and adverse consequences. Finally, the Structured Addictions Assessment Interview for Selecting Therapy (SAAIST; Lightfoot & Hodgins, 1988) is an assessment interview that helps in the selection of therapies based on drug and alcohol use patterns, family and employment environments, and therapy experiences and preferences.

ENHANCING MOTIVATION FOR CHANGE

Introduction

Once the assessment phase is complete and a judgement regarding the suitability of the client for therapy is made, the practitioner can begin working on enhancing motivation for change. The central purpose of this phase is to help the client move to a point where they are committed to changing their drinking behaviour. It is well documented that motivation for change is crucial to successful engagement in therapy. However, a considerable number of clients that present for therapy lack motivation for change or are ambivalent about changing their drinking behaviour. This is widely regarded as a primary obstacle in therapy and is related to a high rate of early dropout.

Therapeutic interventions

The key therapeutic intervention for enhancing motivation for change combines relationship-building principles of non-directive therapy (Rogers, 1961) with specific strategies for resolving ambivalence. This approach, known as motivational interviewing, is based on Miller's (1983) pioneering work that emphasizes the critical importance of the interaction between client and practitioner in modifying ambivalence about changing substance use behaviours. From this perspective, it is fundamental to explore the client's own arguments for change with the role of the practitioner being primarily that of eliciting self-verbalizations reflecting intentions to change, and offering periodic summaries of change talk that the client has put forward.

Additional cognitive exercises (Spada, 2006b) can be used to 'cement' (through reviewing beliefs about change in a systematic manner and in written form) what has emerged from motivational interviewing. These exercises also offer a bridge to the 'action-oriented' phases of therapy that follow.

Working with the client on enhancing motivation for change will thus entail:

- introducing the stages of change model (which is presented below) to outline how the change process works
- employing key motivational interviewing skills and strategies and
- crystallizing progress by summarizing and reviewing what has been explored through the use of cognitive exercises.

In the rest of this section the above skills and strategies will be presented. It is important to note that what follows is only an introduction to the skills and strategies of motivational interviewing. It is thus recommended that the practitioner seeks further training in this area to refine their skills.

Stages of change

The stages of change (or transtheoretical) model by Prochaska and DiClemente (1986) has been widely used in treatment settings as a heuristic for understanding motivation and, more specifically, readiness to change. The model presumes that behaviour change strategies (for example, coping skills training) will only be effective if the client is ready for, and committed to, change. This model postulates that people progress through five stages when changing behaviours: pre-contemplation, contemplation, preparation/determination, action and maintenance.

The pre-contemplation stage
At this stage, the client is unaware of their drinking problem. Alternatively, the client may be thinking about the problematic side of their drinking behaviour but not be concerned about it.

The contemplation stage
At this stage the client may acknowledge the link between drinking and the problems experienced, and may also be trying to work out what is going wrong. This stage is characterized by a period of ambivalence and inaction. At this point it is common for the client to start asking questions such as "Do I have a problem with drinking?" or considering altering their own behaviour "I may have to do something about my drinking".

The preparation/determination stage
At this stage the client begins to perceive a clear discrepancy between current status and desired state. When the balance of advantages and disadvantages for drinking begins to tip towards the direction of change, a

period of preparation ensues that is characterized by exploring change options and making decisions to take action within a proximal time frame. A client may also begin to make small behaviour changes.

The action stage
A serious commitment to action is usually formulated at this stage. The client may decide to change drinking patterns and take practical steps to do so.

The maintenance stage
At this stage the client will be actively trying to implement the proposed actions for change. The focus will be on constantly practising new skills that have been learnt to enable change to crystallize. This should help maintain new habits and behaviours that prevent relapse. The temptation of using alcohol gradually decreases and drinking becomes less central to life. It is an important stage, because if the client has managed to drastically alter their drinking behaviour for a long enough time, they are likely to achieve long-term stability.

Cyclicality

What is important to bear in mind, for both the client and practitioner, is that the process of change is cyclical. In other words, the client goes through the various stages several times before succeeding in dealing with problem drinking. The model implies that the client can re-enter the cycle at any time following a relapse. For example, a client may relapse returning to a pre-contemplative stage by avoiding facing issues they were confronting before lapsing. Or they may return into the cycle at the contemplation stage, asking themselves questions such as "Why did I slip then"; "What happened to my determination, focus and strategies?" There is also a possibility of re-entering at the action stage: "I know what happened and why. I am ready to have a go at tackling the problem now!" Or re-entering at the maintenance stage: "That was a slip and I have already stopped drinking. But I can see that the problems I have had are likely to arise again when I have been abstinent for a long period."

Motivational interviewing skills

The following are the key skills (Miller & Rollnick, 2002) that the practitioner should use when working throughout the process of therapy, but particularly during the initial phases aimed at enhancing motivation for change.

Empathic listening

Discussion about ambivalence, decision-making and behaviour change can be fraught with tension for both client and practitioner. Instead of presenting arguments for change, the practitioner should elicit these from the client. This is not a matter of eliciting these statements and ignoring arguments for not changing, but of giving the client the time to express ambivalence in a setting in which the practitioner's main task is to listen and understand. The use of empathic listening can ensure that the client feels understood and that the practitioner remains in tune with the needs and goals of the client. This involves both simple summary statements (designed to ensure congruence with the client) and more complex statements that enable the practitioner to gradually highlight elements of the client's situation that may encourage resolution of ambivalence. A guideline suggested by practitioners is that one should aim to increase the proportion and accuracy of empathic listening statements and decrease the proportion of direct questions. In the example below a client is engaged in talking about ambivalence. The practitioner's task in employing empathic listening is not to get ahead to any other topic but simply to allow the client to explore the ambivalence.

Practitioner: Have you noticed anything about the effect of drinking on your feelings?
Client: Yes, I have. It numbs them. Drinking allows me to take a break from what I dislike feeling: bored, low and angry.
Practitioner: Drinking takes over then.
Client: Yes, and it is good. I could have felt low but it gives me the chance to not care about these feelings.
Practitioner: It is a shield. Is it a good one too?
Client: For a while at least. Eventually I will feel upset again about something, small things, and then I get more upset. The feelings won't go away.
Practitioner: So drinking can give you a lift but you still get those lows in mood.
Client: That's right. You cannot imagine how I feel the next day: In the doldrums. What a life of ups and downs and nothing other than alcohol to help! I can't take this anymore.

Responding to resistance

Resistance can be described as arising when the practitioner loses congruence with the client. It can be conceived of as an opposition to the practitioner and as a general reluctance to make progress. Responding constructively to resistance is crucially important in the early stages of the therapeutic encounter, when the possibilities of misunderstanding and tension are very common. Being open about the practitioner's role as well as focusing on the client's agenda can go a long way towards diffusing misunderstanding and tension. One of the most common errors that practitioners make is to presume greater levels of readiness for change than are actually being experienced by the client. Similarly there may be a tendency to focus primarily on drinking behaviour when the client is equally if not more concerned about some other problem area. The outcome will be a weakened rapport, low motivation and disengagement. Responding to resistance effectively will entail genuinely reflecting and acknowledging the client's need to preserve dignity and to be heard, thereby weakening the oppositional nature of the interaction. Empathic listening remains the most useful way of doing this. In the example below, the practitioner initially focuses on a drinking problem, which in response elicits resistance from an upset client. The practitioner proceeds to rectify the oppositional nature of the interaction by using empathic listening.

Practitioner: It appears that the key reason you are here is to address your problematic drinking behaviour, is that right?

Client: Not really: Actually no. This is typical isn't it? You sound just like my husband. It is all about drinking, drinking, and more drinking. That's the reason behind everything. Well if all you want to do is talk about drinking, then I may as well quit now.

Practitioner: It appears that for you there is a lot more than just a possible issue with drinking. Other things are bothering you.

Client: Yes. I get told time and time again that my drinking is the problem and that nothing else matters. It is just not right.

Practitioner: Other things are also important and it is clear that you don't want them to be put aside.

Client: That's correct. I've had enough of people wanting me to put them aside. I want to talk about these things.

Practitioner: Taking your time, and if you so wish, tell me about other important things that matter.

Developing discrepancy

In the exploration of the client's personal values and aspirations for the future, which is one of the central motivational interviewing strategies, discrepancy (a state of discomfort) can arise from the contrast between the client's goals and their current situation. This realization should not be viewed as something to be avoided but as a catalyst for change. The development of discrepancy will allow the client to see how their problem drinking might be at odds with what is important to them and their hopes in the future.

As will be described in the following section, the practitioner will have to prompt the client by asking predominantly open-ended questions and by using empathic listening, with a view to engendering discrepancy. It is important to always avoid pressing the client to give 'right' answers and to reflect both sides of the argument for continuing or giving up problem drinking.

Supporting self-efficacy

Self-efficacy can be defined as the specific belief that one is able to perform a particular task or behaviour (Bandura, 1997). Often a client expresses rather negative and pessimistic views of being able to cope with their problem drinking. Statements such as "I tried to stop in the past but have never succeeded" or "My drinking is uncontrollable" are very common. Throughout the course of therapy, but especially early on, helping the client to develop a sense that they can cope with the situation will be of benefit to them. It is important to elicit inner conviction rather than imposing it from without, and to display optimism about behavioural change.

Motivational interviewing strategies

The following strategies (Miller & Rollnick, 2002) should always be delivered through the use of the core motivational skills highlighted in the previous section.

Exploration of the good and less good aspects of alcohol use

It is important to begin by allowing the client to explore their own thoughts and feelings about alcohol use. The practitioner must be non-judgemental and avoid responses that might be interpreted by the client as disapproval or surprise about the definition of what is 'good' or 'less good' about alcohol use. By focusing on the good things about the person's alcohol use, the practitioner is helping to build trust. Open questions include:

"What are the good things about your drinking?"
"How does drinking help?"
"What do you like about drinking?"

The practitioner should then acknowledge and summarize all the good things without over-emphasizing them:

"Some of the positive reasons you are drinking are. . ."

The client should then be probed to identify the less good aspects of alcohol use. The practitioner should avoid using strong expressions, e.g. 'bad things' or 'problems' unless the client uses this language first. Open questions include:

"What are the less good things about your drinking?"
"What are the things you do not like so much about your drinking?"

Again, the practitioner will need to remain non-judgemental as well as follow up exploratory questions with more specific open-ended questions:

"So how does this affect you?"
"Where does that leave you?"

It is important to ensure that the client's meaning is really understood and not taken literally. If the client says something like "I am worried about my health", the practitioner will need to follow up with something like: "Can you give me an example of when . . . can you tell me a bit more about that. . .?"

Exploration of concerns about alcohol use
Less good things are not necessarily matters of concern for the client. It is therefore important to clarify which matters are of concern to the client. More open-ended questions are required, such as:

"How do you feel about that?"
"Is that a problem or concern for you in any way?"

Emphasizing in this way and further exploring concerns is of central importance. In exploring concerns, the skills of empathic listening and summarizing are fundamental: they will reinforce the client's own concern through repetition. Other ways to raise issues and concerns include asking the client how they saw themselves in the past and what they would like to see for themselves in the future:

"How does that differ from what is happening now?"
"How do you feel about that?"
"What effect did drinking have on your life?"

Moving on to:

"How would you like things to be different in the future?"
"What is stopping you doing what you would like to do?"

After this exploration the practitioner should summarize past/future aspirations in relation to the present, emphasizing the role of alcohol use. The practitioner should try to use the client's own words as much as possible. A likely outcome of this phase is that the client will feel hopeless – it is therefore essential that the practitioner stresses the possibility of change and a better life. At this point the practitioner may want to begin addressing the client's discrepancy between the person and the problem drinker. Key probes:

"How would you describe the things you like about yourself?"

This should be followed by reflective listening and a summary. Moving on to:

"And how would you describe yourself as the alcohol user?"

After this exploration phase the practitioner should summarize as far as possible the client's words. For example:

"It seems that on the one hand you like . . . and on the other hand. . ."

Initial decision-making
This stage aims to help the client make a decision to commit to change. The client is ready to move to this stage if there is decreased resistance, and there are fewer questions about the problem and more about change. The types of questions used include:

"Where does this leave us now?"
"What does this mean about your alcohol use?"

When the client states that they want to reduce their alcohol use, the practitioner must not take over and tell them what to do. It is possible, at this point, to introduce the client to the crucial role that case formulation plays in understanding the mechanics of their problem. It is also the point to begin facilitating goal setting, starting with exploration of the vaguer goals of change with the aim of transforming them into more concrete ones:

Table 2.2 A drinking decisional balance sheet

Continuing to drink		Making a change to my drinking	
Benefits	Costs	Benefits	Costs
Helps me relax Makes me feel good	Damages my health Is expensive Makes me feel low It is hurting my partner	Feeling better Happier marriage More cash	Will I still be liked? Will I still have fun? How will I relax? How will I switch off?

"How would your life be different if you followed this idea and quit altogether?"
"Have you said that you think you would like to cut down? How would it work?"
"What are some of the skills you have now that might help you achieve your goal?"

Cognitive strategies

Following the initial exploratory motivational work, it is useful for both client and practitioner to summarize in written form what has been discussed. The following exercises are designed to do this and can be undertaken as an out-of-therapy session activity.

Completing a drinking decisional balance sheet

This involves making a list of the advantages and disadvantages of continuing to drink or making a change to drinking habits. It is important the client records their own advantages and disadvantages. This task is helpful in cementing the progress achieved through motivational exercises and allows the client to examine the issue from a number of different perspectives. This should also help the client have a more accurate, objective and balanced view of their drinking problem. Statements generated from this strategy can be used as material for other strategies, such as flashcards, and may be particularly helpful in goal setting. A completed drinking decisional balance sheet is presented in Table 2.2.

Reiterating problems and goals

At this stage it is important to provide a client with a summary of:

⊙ the drinking problem as reflected in their self-motivational statements
⊙ the nature of their ambivalence (including what remains positive about the drinking) and
⊙ any indications offered of wanting, intending or planning to change

Table 2.3 Problems and goals

Problems	Goals
Drinking has resulted in health and relationship problems	Abstinence
Drinking results in unwanted fights	Abstinence
Drinking has resulted in a limited range and amount of social or recreational activities	Increase the number of pleasurable activities each week, including individual exercise, reading or listening to music. This should help me realize that a sober life is not boring!

In order to give greater concreteness to what has been discussed, it is fundamental to summarize problems and set goals. Both problems and goals will be further reviewed in the case formulation phase and during the course of therapy, so it is important to make clear to the client that they may well change over time. Table 2.3 shows a completed exercise identifying problems and goals.

Tackling concerns about change
It is inevitable that the client will experience concerns about giving up or changing their drinking behaviour. Some of these concerns will have been highlighted in the drinking decisional balance sheet and through the motivational interviewing process. Amongst the most common concerns presented is that stopping drinking or changing one's drinking patterns will expose an empty life, lead to unbearable craving episodes or an impossibility to cope with difficulties. The reality is that many clients will present moderate difficulties in shifting their thoughts to other matters or occupying their time with other activities, managing to cope more effectively than originally thought with both craving and the pressures of life. For some clients, however, it may not be so straightforward to 'get going' again, and life may appear to be extremely empty and lonely without alcohol. This is more likely to be the case if the client does not have an adequate social support system. The practitioner will therefore need to emphasize to the client that changing drinking habits will go hand in hand with building alternative coping skills and reward structures. The message to put across is that the client will not be left without support. The following exercise (see Table 2.4) is designed to further cement commitment to change by looking in greater detail at the advantages and disadvantages of changing together with responses to concerns. This exercise will help the client weigh up whether any of these concerns about change are realistic or not.

Table 2.4 Advantages of changing, concerns of changing and responses to concerns

Advantages	Concerns	Responses to concerns
Get a job that I deserve, that will make me feel good about myself Fewer money problems Chance to be a decent partner	Cravings will overcome me	I have ridden out cravings in the past. There is evidence I can do it again. As my motivation to stop drinking has increased, so will my ability to resist cravings
Chance to feel good more consistently Family will be pleased and worry less	I'll always have cravings for alcohol	I no longer have cravings for nicotine although I did for a while. It is likely to be the same for alcohol
I'll be able to take responsibility for my life (e.g. finances, career, relationships, self-development and health)	I'll always miss the highs	The highs are obviously not worth it and it is unlikely that I'll always miss them. I don't miss nicotine although I did for a while when I first gave it up. It is likely to be the same with alcohol. I may miss it for a year or so, and then I won't think about it much
Outcome		
I can get through the cravings and they will not last forever. Alcohol results in solitary bingeing and unwanted behaviour and thoughts. My life could be much more interesting and full if I stop drinking. I can have a largely pleasurable and productive life without alcohol and most people don't care whether I drink or not		

Examining specific change concerns

The final exercise in this section (see Table 2.5) is designed to help the client estimate how realistic any concerns they have about change may be. This will help them to get a better idea about what stopping drinking or changing drinking patterns will mean or will achieve in practice, and whether they will need to prepare, with the practitioner, a detailed plan to deal with any problems that may result.

At this stage a client may already have a drinking goal in mind (abstinence or controlled drinking). Whatever drinking goal is chosen is legitimate. That said, evidence shows that controlled drinking is more difficult than abstaining. Abstaining is straightforward – the client has to just avoid drinking alcohol. Controlled drinking, however, is open to deliberate or accidental miscalculation of how much one may have drunk. In addition, it should be remembered that alcohol has a disinhibitory

Table 2.5 Examining specific change concerns

What do you predict will happen?	
My life will become boring and empty	
How likely is it to happen (0–100%)? 50%	
Evidence for	Evidence against
I sometimes feel bored or low when I don't drink Drinking is often a part of many social activities. How will I cope without it?	After I've been drinking, I feel extremely low for long periods of time. I may feel better without drinking If I drink, I am unable to have a relationship If I drink, I diminish my capacity to have a productive life. This means that I will continue to feel bored
Outcome How likely do you think it is now that this will happen? (0–100%) 30%	
Conclusions I am more likely to have an interesting and full life without alcohol than with it	

effect, which could mean that even if the client feels totally certain they will keep to a prearranged limit before drinking, they may not once the first units have been drunk. Some clients appear more successful at pursuing a controlled drinking goal than others. They usually (but not always) tend to be younger, in employment, with a family around them, have a short history of drinking problems, lower consumption levels before seeking help, and show no signs of physical dependence. In the following section drinking goals will be discussed as an integral part of the case formulation. It is important to bear in mind the points just raised.

CASE FORMULATION

Introduction

Once the enhancement of motivation phase is initiated and the client's motivation for change is strengthened, therapy will naturally progress towards the case formulation phase. The central purpose of case formulation is to develop a model, or clinical theory, that can explain how the drinking problem and associated problems developed and are maintained, and consequently how therapeutic interventions should be selected, delivered and sequenced. The case formulation protocol presented is adapted from the University College London (UCL) case formulation paradigm (Bruch & Bond, 1998). It will be illustrated in more detail below and in the case example presented in Chapter 5.

Defining problems

Case formulation begins by exploring with the client his/her general views and expectations about CBT. Early on it may be useful to explain the rationale and procedure of CBT, emphasizing, in particular, active participation, goal orientation and therapy as a continuous learning process. This phase is entirely client-centred and its aim is to obtain a comprehensive subjective statement of the drinking problem and associated problems (description, development and coping resources), desired outcomes of therapy (goals), as well as reasons for seeking therapeutic help at this time.

The information provided in this phase should facilitate an operationalization of the drinking problem and associated problems, which will be investigated in the next phase. A special emphasis should also be placed on identifying factors that contributed to previous therapy successes or failures. This can be achieved through a series of open-ended questions, including some of the following:

"Have you received any therapy for problem drinking before? When was that?"
"Can you tell me a little bit more about it?"
"What did you like or not like about the programme?"
"What do you think made it successful/unsuccessful?"
"Have you had any periods of abstinence or controlled drinking? When was the last one? Can you tell me a little bit more about that period?"
"What do you think helped you to maintain the abstinence or control over your drinking?"

Exploring problems

This phase is led and structured by the practitioner with the aim of refining further initial hypotheses of cause and maintenance, and achieving a comprehensive conceptualization of the drinking problem and associated problems. Functional and developmental analyses should be carried out in order to gain a full understanding of the different stimulus conditions for alcohol use and how they coalesce into the drinking problem.

Functional analysis

A functional analysis involves building hypotheses regarding the function, or purpose, of target behaviours. Through this tool both client and practitioner can develop a more detailed understanding of the 'mechanics' of behaviour:

⊙ the most frequent and potent antecedents of it
⊙ the short-term positive consequences that serve to maintain it and
⊙ the long-term costs of continuing to engage in it

The specific typology of functional analysis used in this book is based on Goldfried and Sprafkin's (1976) Stimulus-Organism-Response-Consequence (S-O-R-C) model of behaviour. This model purports that any behaviour (response) is a function of the environment, the organism (or person) and the consequences of the behaviour. The S-O-R-C model thus includes antecedent stimuli (S), factors inherent to the organism (O), a target response (R) and consequences (C). It suggests that a stimulus (S) will act on the organism (O) to emit behaviour (R) when certain reinforcing consequences (C) occur. The stimulus refers to any event that will trigger a given behaviour. In the case of problem drinking, this can include particular environments, thoughts, physiological sensations or emotional states. The organism refers to individual differences in biological factors, experience and learning. For example, individual differences in biological make-up may make alcohol more or less reinforcing to the person. Importantly, however, at an organism level, cognitive constructs such as expectancies, beliefs, self-perceptions and attention play a crucial role in determining the choice of response. Responses can be defined as verbal responses, physical responses or expressed actions. In the case of problem drinking this will mean using alcohol, or initiating behaviours aimed at using it, as well as the frequency and duration of use. Consequences are events or results which support or obstruct a given response; for example, alcohol use temporarily reducing negative emotion (a 'maintaining' consequence) but causing a lowering of mood in the longer term (a 'problem' consequence).

This S-O-R-C model therefore caters for current environmental stimuli and consequences as well as individual differences and learning history. A quadripartite response system analysis is built into this design to allow the study of individual response modalities in a methodical manner. According to the model, once problem behaviour and its functional relationships have been identified, therapeutic interventions may be identified and implemented.

An example of the model in action (see Figure 2.1) would be being in a pub and experiencing social discomfort (S), activating positive expectancies about alcohol and craving (O), which in turn would elicit drinking (R). The latter would be reinforced (short-term maintaining consequences) primarily by a reduction in craving and social discomfort (C). In the long term, a variety of problem consequences would emerge (e.g. negative beliefs about uncontrollability of alcohol use, negative beliefs about the self regarding social interaction and negative emotion), which would, in turn, act as stimuli for further drinking episodes. Continuing from the example above, controlling stimulus conditions (e.g. reducing the frequency of pub visits), cognitive restructuring of positive expectancies, distraction exercises for dealing with craving and the enhancement of coping skills (e.g. interpersonal skills, drinking refusal skills and managing negative emotion) are therapeutic interventions that could be implemented as they are consistent with the functional relationships identified.

A second example of the model in action (see Figure 2.2) could begin from one of the problem consequences identified in the first functional analysis. The stimulus (S) could be experiencing an episode of negative emotion at home, which in turn may activate positive expectancies and craving (O) leading to drinking (R). The latter would be reinforced (short-term maintaining consequences) by the improvement of negative emotion and reduction of craving (C). In the long term, a variety of problem consequences would emerge (e.g. negative beliefs about the self concerning trait-like problem drinking behaviour, and an escalation of negative emotion). Continuing from the example above, the enhancement of coping skills (e.g. scheduling alternative activities and managing negative emotion), cognitive restructuring of positive expectancies and distraction exercises for dealing with craving are all therapeutic interventions that could be implemented as they are consistent with the functional relationships identified. Functional analyses can also be transposed into flow charts or diagrammatic representations. This may help the client visualize the different stages of a given drinking problem and grasp better its perseverative nature. An example of a flow chart derived from the first functional analysis (Figure 2.1) is presented in Figure 2.3.

Integrated developmental profiling

The objective of this phase is to develop a more detailed and integrated understanding of predisposing factors, circumstances of onset, as well as historic triggers and maintenance factors underlying the drinking problem and associated problems. Some of the information needed to develop such an understanding may already be available, having been acquired through the assessment process and the definition of problems. Typically, the developmental analysis will reveal marked differences between onset and later manifestations of problem drinking and shed light on the interactions between different stimulus conditions. This, in turn, will help to determine their role and relative importance. The emphasis should be on experiences relevant to the development of problem drinking behaviour and associated problems, such as:

- When and how did the client start drinking?
- How did the initial use lead to the present problematic drinking patterns?
- What prevented the client from being able to change or stop using alcohol in an unhelpful way?
- How did key beliefs develop?
- What are the associated problems and how do they relate to the problem drinking patterns?

The problem formulation

The systematic gathering of information through the definition and exploration of problems, functional analyses and integrated developmental profiling will promote the gradual formation of a comprehensive 'clinical theory': the problem formulation. In this phase, the practitioner should attempt to gather all information available into a coherent narrative. A problem formulation is an attempt to explain how the client's drinking problem functions, why and how it developed and what maintains it. The problem formulation also allows predictions to be outlined (based on individual functional analyses) and consequently therapeutic intervention hypotheses to be delineated. The problem formulation can be pictured, in part, as bringing together different functional analyses through a concatenation (or chain) process, where the responses and problem consequences arising from one functional analysis become the stimuli for a further functional analysis or set of functional analyses, seamlessly linking all functional analyses together. A diagrammatic example of a problem formulation where different functional analyses

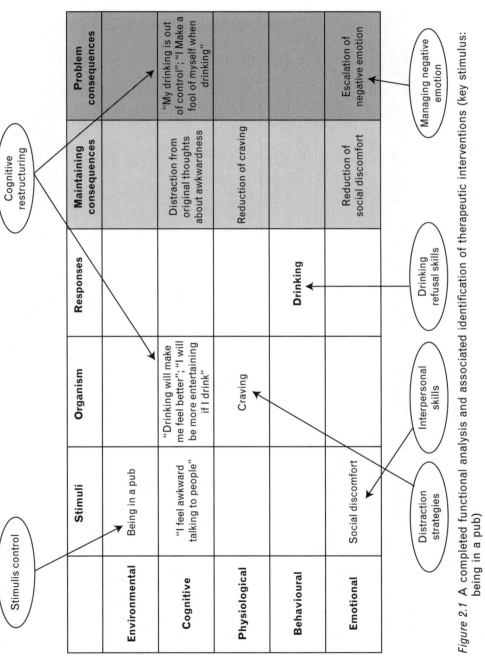

Figure 2.1 A completed functional analysis and associated identification of therapeutic interventions (key stimulus: being in a pub)

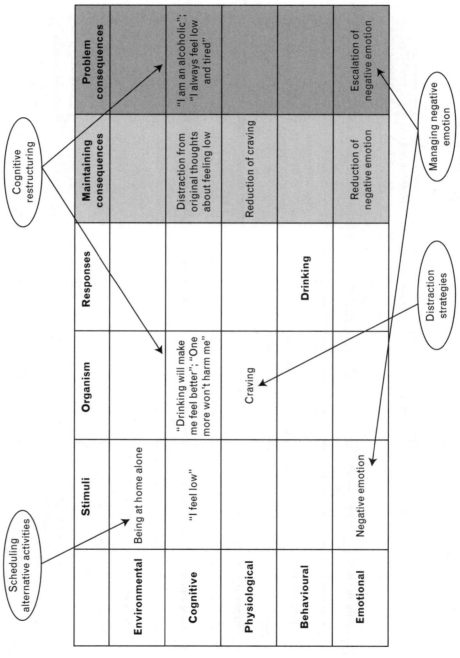

Figure 2.2 A completed functional analysis and associated identification of therapeutic intervention (key stimulus: being at home alone)

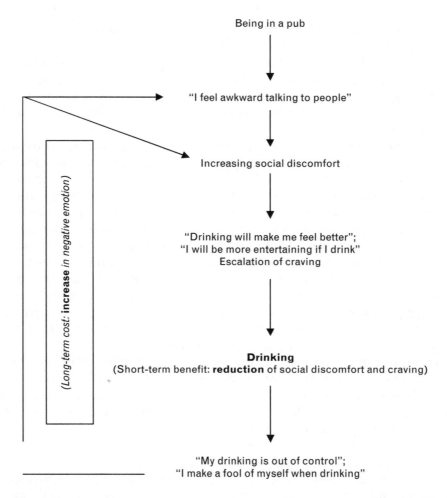

Being in a pub

"I feel awkward talking to people"

Increasing social discomfort

"Drinking will make me feel better";
"I will be more entertaining if I drink"
Escalation of craving

Drinking
(Short-term benefit: **reduction** of social discomfort and craving)

"My drinking is out of control";
"I make a fool of myself when drinking"

(Long-term cost: **increase** *in negative emotion)*

Figure 2.3 A transposition of a functional analysis (from Figure 2.1) into a model

are linked is presented in Figure 2.4. In this example, the integrated developmental profiling indicated that problematic drinking behaviour started in social settings and then extended to drinking alone. Eventually it led to problems with self-esteem and increasing perseveration of drinking behaviour. The problem formulation presented links four functional analyses of drinking behaviour that have been developed in conjunction with the developmental history of the problem. In this analysis, it was identified that drinking (R1) started initially as a means of coping with social discomfort (S1), which gradually led to an escalation of negative emotion (PC1) as a problem consequence. Negative emotion (PC1) then progressively became a trigger (S2) for drinking (R2) also when alone, which slowly gave rise to moderate withdrawal (PC2) as a problem consequence. Moderate withdrawal then became a trigger (S3) for further drinking (R3), which led to a reduction in self-esteem (PC3), because of absenteeism at work, as a problem consequence. Low self-esteem then became a trigger (S4) for further drinking (R4), which locked the individual in a vicious cycle (PC4).

From the above problem formulation and individual functional analyses, an initial plan of therapeutic interventions can be designed. Central to this would be motivational interventions, the management of craving (as drinking appears to have become perseverative) and the bolstering of coping skills (e.g. drinking refusal skills). The restructuring of outcome expectancies about the benefits of drinking in regulating negative emotion would also feature prominently as the individual is using alcohol, in part, to manage social discomfort. Interventions aimed at ensuring the individual returns to work would also be important to bolster self-esteem and improve mood, which in turn would help to interrupt perseveration in alcohol use. Interventions aimed at identifying the roots of social discomfort (lack of social skills, fear of negative evaluation, etc.) would also be included in therapy.

It is important to share and discuss the problem formulation, including any therapeutic intervention hypotheses, before embarking on the therapy itself. This is done to increase motivation through transparency and to lay the ground for the client to become an active partner in therapy. The following guidelines can aid this process:

⊙ explaining the purpose and rationale of a problem formulation
⊙ explaining the mechanisms underlying the drinking problem and associated problems
⊙ explaining how the drinking problem has developed using examples from the developmental analysis
⊙ emphasizing that the drinking problem is understood predominantly as a series of learned responses, which can be subject to modification employing the same principles
⊙ outlining a range of therapeutic intervention options arising from the individual functional analyses and the problem formulation, including the advantages and disadvantages for each option
⊙ concluding whether an appropriate therapy programme can be offered
⊙ inviting comments from the client on all the above points and asking the client to spend a week or so considering the problem formulation and therapy implications

In conclusion, the case formulation is designed to provide active guidance for all further steps in therapy, in particular regarding the selection and sequencing of therapeutic interventions. Case formulation enables the

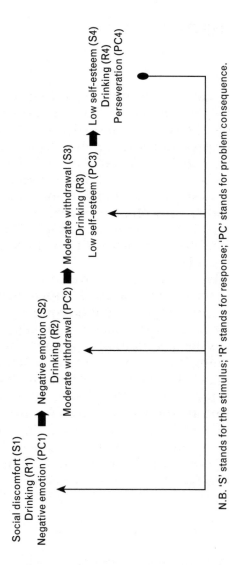

N.B. 'S' stands for the stimulus; 'R' stands for response; 'PC' stands for problem consequence.

Figure 2.4 A diagrammatic representation of a problem formulation

practitioner and client to understand how individual predisposition, learning processes, environmental factors and associated problems interact with each other to giving rise to the drinking problem being presented.

KEY ISSUES IN THERAPY

Introduction

CBT for problem drinking can be broadly divided into three phases. The first phase is aimed at helping the client become motivated and committed to change. Part of this is accomplished through the assessment and case formulation processes and part through dedicated motivational exercises. The second phase focuses on helping the client initiate early changes in behaviour. These have to be introduced and practised for a minimum of 12 therapy sessions (3 months) and ideally longer (24 therapy sessions or 6 months). This phase is crucial as a large proportion of relapses occur within the first 3 months of therapy. The third phase is aimed at reviewing what the client has achieved, what needs to be worked on and how to maintain change.

In this book, the first phase of therapy is covered in chapter 2, 'Preparing for Change', and the second in chapter 3, 'Implementing Change'. Ideally, in the latter section, one topic should be covered in an individual therapy session, especially in the early stages of therapy. However, the number of therapy sessions devoted to each topic, and the order of topic delivery, may vary according to the needs of the client and the case formulation. The final phase of therapy is covered in chapter 4, 'Maintaining Change'. Some of the topics in this chapter may be incorporated into the therapy programme as required, and need not necessarily be kept until all the topics in chapter 3, 'Implementing Change', have been covered. It is, however, advisable to follow the order of chapters and topics as suggested in the book (with flexibility on the number of therapy sessions allocated per topic).

Structure of therapy sessions

There is no recommended number of therapy sessions proven to be related to positive outcomes. However, in consideration of the high relapse rates observed within the first 3 months of therapy, it makes sense that each client should receive at least 12 therapy sessions 50 minutes in duration. Each therapy session should be divided into three parts. The second part, usually the longest one lasting for 20 minutes, will address the current topic. The first and third parts of the therapy session, which should be around 15 minutes in duration, are the same for all therapy sessions. The therapy session structure should be adhered to even if the same topic is covered on more than one occasion. Structure is important for a variety of reasons:

⊙ it helps to develop and maintain a collaborative component in therapy
⊙ it allows for the best use of allocated time
⊙ it helps the client to experience what structure feels like during the therapy
⊙ it acknowledges the importance of out-of-therapy session assignments and
⊙ it emphasizes control, prediction and planning

Part 1 of the therapy session

After welcoming and making the client feel at ease, the practitioner should introduce the therapy session by agreeing to its duration, and reminding the client about its structure and format. If this is the first therapy session, or there has been a break for a period of time, this introduction is very important.

The key areas to cover in this part of the therapy include:

⊙ briefly reviewing life issues since the last therapy session, for example episodes of problem drinking, craving and triggers. This review should be brief and become the bridge for the next step
⊙ eliciting current concerns/problems. This is fundamental in order to maintain and reinforce the therapeutic relationship. It may also determine what is going to be covered in the therapy session, especially in the case of a new problem or if a crisis arises
⊙ briefly reviewing topics covered in the previous therapy sessions and reviewing what was agreed for the current therapy session. In this way the concept of continuity and the importance of achieving small steps are simultaneously emphasized
⊙ briefly reviewing out-of-therapy session assignments that had been allocated for that week
⊙ agreeing an agenda for the therapy session (i.e. topic to be covered)

It is important to remember that therapy is a fluid and collaborative process. What was agreed following assessment and case formulation is important, but what is most important is what the client brings to the therapy session, the meaning the client attributes to what is happening in their life and the therapy process itself.

Part 2 of the therapy session

This part of the therapy session is described in detail under the separate topic headings in the next two chapters ('Implementing Change' and 'Maintaining Change'). The importance of continuity of therapy and concordance of topics discussed in the case formulation should be emphasized.

Part 3 of the therapy session

If all previous steps have been covered, there should be enough time to summarize and prepare for the week to come. Out-of-therapy session assignments are a very important part of therapy. In order to encourage the client to practise new skills and behaviours, they must be able to understand why it is crucial to do so. It is also fundamental for the client to have written instructions and to make a note of the agreed tasks. The tasks need to be clear and specific. It is advisable not to allocate too many tasks and to make clear links with the therapy session. It is also important to bear in mind that usually the best assignments are the ones proposed and undertaken by the client themselves, with the practitioner only there to facilitate review and learning from them.

Therapy goals

CBT for problem drinking does not require total abstinence as a precondition or a necessity for successful outcomes. Indeed, because there is an emphasis in CBT on matching therapeutic interventions to specific client characteristics and needs, flexibility in the selection of therapeutic goals is advocated. Although individual practitioners may vary in the degree to which they insist on an abstinence goal for their client, there is a substantial body of literature suggesting that many individuals with problem drinking, particularly those who are not dependent and have strong social support systems, can and do become moderate drinkers often without any therapeutic input.

CBT practitioners will typically work with a client incrementally toward abstinence and its maintenance, if that is what the client insists on, and if the client's level of alcohol consumption does not carry with it a risk of immediate and catastrophic consequences. The process of goal determination is one of negotiation rather than practitioner insistence. This is consistent with the notion that the more committed the client is to a particular goal, the greater the likelihood of reaching it.

Measurement

To enable a comprehensive evaluation of the therapeutic interventions, measures of improvement should be collected. These measures can refer to short-term vs long-term improvements, specific vs global adjustment, and client vs expert estimates. Furthermore, they should be judged in the short term (in therapy session), as well as the long term (e.g. follow-up). Finally, there should be an assessment as to whether any changes are relating to symptomatic complaints as well as to life adjustment indicators.

Measures for these dimensions will typically include subjective ratings and questionnaires (such as those highlighted in 'Assessment', page 18). Depending on the complexity and length of any therapy programme, a chosen set of measures is employed before, during and after therapy, as well as for several follow-up occasions. The emphasis on measurement is on evaluation of therapeutic change as opposed to diagnostic or psychometric assessment. When using standardized measures, it may be an added benefit to compare individual data with relevant groups.

Multidimensional measurements are useful in determining a profile for outcome and change. For example, converging evidence for positive changes may indicate overall sustained improvements, whereas discrepant measures may indicate isolated or even disputable gains. Obviously, there must be concern when improvements with symptomatic complaints do not correlate with improved life adjustment, or when the client and practitioner do not agree on crucial outcome measures. Conversely, convergence on all measures would strongly endorse the problem formulation and the therapy programme.

Compliance with therapy

Lack of compliance with therapy is a common obstacle when working with problem drinkers. This is because such clients have typically experienced social stigma and judgemental behaviour from the wider social context. They may also have a misguided understanding of therapeutic interventions, which can be due to reluctance to enquire openly and ask for help. Typically, reluctance is associated with a number of issues including:

⊙ issues of confidentiality
⊙ access to medical records by insurance or other companies

⊙ lack of information available and incorrect, out-of-date information given by health professionals and
⊙ negative experiences with prior therapy or relapse

The practitioner can explore the above issues during the assessment and case formulation phases or later on during therapy (when and if poor compliance is manifested).

Lateness and non-attendance are common problems in chaotic problem drinkers, which can hinder the progress of therapy. The practitioner should discuss ground rules with the client at the beginning of the therapy, which should include:

⊙ the importance of regular attendance
⊙ being in time for therapy sessions and
⊙ communicating absences in advance and re-scheduling appointments

Despite this, some clients fail to attend (and notify absence and re-schedule appointments) or are late. This may be particularly common in the early stages of therapy when the client is typically ambivalent about changing their behaviour, so the practitioner should explore the reasons for lateness and/or non-attendance. Common reasons for non-attendance will include practical issues such as childcare or difficulties getting to therapy. The practitioner may need to use (and re-use) motivational strategies and explore the client's ambivalent feelings about therapy and reasons for non-compliance.

Finally, arriving intoxicated should be discussed in the ground rules at the outset of therapy. Generally, the therapy session should be cancelled and re-scheduled, and the practitioner should ensure the client arrives home safely. However, arriving intoxicated may be a sign the client has experienced a crisis, so even if it is not explored at the time, it should be explored in the next scheduled therapy session.

The therapeutic relationship

Research has distinguished between common and unique factors of therapy. Common factors relate to dimensions of therapy that are shared across most psychotherapeutic approaches. These include psycho-education, support, expectations of improvement, an experienced therapist, and the quality of the therapeutic relationship. Of all these factors, the therapeutic relationship has emerged as the key predictor of positive outcomes (Lambert & Ogles, 2004).

Several studies have investigated the role of the therapeutic relationship in the therapy of problem drinking. This is a particularly important factor given the ambivalence most clients have with respect to changing their drinking behaviour. Evidence suggests that a better therapeutic relationship early in therapy may prevent dropout and facilitate client engagement (e.g. Meier, Barrowclough, & Donmall, 2005).

Meier et al. (2005) have found that clients with higher readiness to change, more successful relationship histories, a secure attachment style, and better social support find it easier to establish successful therapeutic relationships. However, because many problem drinkers do not have good social support, lack adequate coping skills and are ambivalent about changing their behaviour, the practitioner may need to invest extra time and effort in establishing a therapeutic relationship.

What will contribute to a good therapeutic relationship? As a general rule, the practitioner should work with the client without preconceived ideas about needs and goals. By accepting the client's definition of the problem, the practitioner will in effect meet their needs. This in turn will facilitate the development of a productive relationship. A collaborative stance aimed at working toward shared goals is also likely to strengthen the therapeutic relationship. Further, the therapeutic style should be flexible and adaptable to the needs of the client in the specific phase of the therapeutic process.

Implementing change

DEALING WITH STIMULUS CONDITIONS

Introduction

Stimulus conditions (or activating events) are situations in which the client encounters stimuli that are likely to trigger alcohol use. The nature of these stimuli can vary considerably, but they broadly fall into two categories: internal (e.g. low mood) and external (e.g. a pub). It is important to begin by explaining to the client that "a stimulus condition is any situation that poses a threat to your sense of control and increases the risk of using alcohol".

Identifying stimulus conditions

The practitioner and client should then attempt to develop a list of all stimulus conditions by:

◉ referring to the assessment and case formulation phases where key stimuli conditions will have been identified
◉ referring to recent examples of use (e.g. over the past two weeks)
◉ discussing previous lapses and identifying triggers and
◉ using hypothetical case scenarios of what could lead to a lapse

Factors that may typically trigger alcohol use will include: hunger and thirst, people, availability of money and alcohol, the place where the drinking takes place, the time of the day and day of the week, and emotional states. Some of these key triggers are explored in more detail below.

People

Certain individuals can make it more likely for the client to begin using alcohol. People who drink heavily, ridicule moderation, push drinks or buy rounds are likely to increase the client's chances of using alcohol. In other cases, drinking patterns may be affected by the way the client feels around certain people. For example, some individuals may make the client anxious, with drinking providing a way to relax. Sometimes drinking simply happens because of what the client does with a particular person. If, for example, the client is friends with an individual who likes to go from pub to pub, it will be harder to avoid drinking. Conversely, there are going to be other individuals who the client is more likely to drink moderately with or not drink with at all. These will include moderate drinkers, abstainers or simply people that the client does not feel anxious with. There may be times the client will also restrain their alcohol consumption to make a favourable impression (e.g. with a boss, a doctor, etc.). It is useful to ask the client to record who affects their drinking and how.

Places

It may be instantly obvious to both practitioner and client what high-risk drinking places are, but it can also be subtle. For example, individuals are more likely to drink heavily in places where:

- certain kinds of music are played
- competition is high for sexual partners
- other people are drinking heavily and
- the lights are turned down

Again, the practitioner should attempt to elicit these more subtle environmental cues and ask the client to record them.

Time

Another key factor that can affect drinking patterns is time. Most people who over-drink will do so on certain days of the week and at certain times of the day. Evenings, weekends, holidays and special occasions (such as parties and weddings) are likely to involve heavier drinking.

Recording stimulus conditions

A detailed recording system is needed in order to identify stimulus conditions (activating events) and observe how they are interlinked. An example of a completed exercise aimed at monitoring activating events is presented in Table 3.1.

Table 3.1 Activating event breakdown

Date	Time	Drink	Amount	Situation	Thoughts	Emotion
05/09/06	19:30	Wine	2 glasses	At home before going out to meet new people at a party	"Will I be liked?"; "A drink takes the edge off"	Apprehension
07/09/06	20:00	Wine	5 glasses	Talking to people at the restaurant	"I don't like these people", "Why am I wasting my time and money with them?"	Frustration Boredom
07/09/06	23:00	Whiskey	2 shots	At home alone	"Another wasted evening!"	Anger Loneliness

Noting over a period of a few weeks how different situations, thoughts and emotions bring about drinking will help the client identify patterns of activating events that will:

⊙ extend what has been investigated during the pre-therapy phase when undertaking functional analyses of drinking behaviours and
⊙ provide insight into further areas to be tackled in therapy

As with the case formulation, it is important to bear in mind that functional analyses are dynamic and can be modified and updated throughout the course of therapy. Indeed, it is difficult to gather all relevant data in the pre-therapy phase as well as cover all possible triggers for alcohol use. This is why recording stimulus conditions in therapy is an essential step in cementing the understanding of the 'mechanics' of alcohol use for a given client.

Dealing with stimulus conditions

The next step is to help the client in exploring how to cope with stimulus conditions. It is essential to review the client's existing coping strategies, which will have already, to an extent, been identified through the functional analyses. Following this, an outline of how stimulus conditions are typically dealt with can be put forward. This will include learning how to:

1 avoid the stimulus conditions altogether
2 cope by confronting the stimulus conditions and resisting using alcohol by modifying cognitions relating to alcohol use, tackling craving and developing a generic coping plan for when the situation arises.

Later sections in this book will cover areas detailed in point 2. It is important to emphasize that the ultimate aim is to enable the client to cope with stimulus conditions because avoidance is not always possible. In earlier stages of therapy, however, avoidance may be the only option until the client has developed a sufficiently solid repertoire of skills that will allow them to respond adaptively to triggers for alcohol use.

The following basic strategies can be employed early on to break old associations between stimulus conditions and drinking if avoidance is not an option:

⦿ if going out, take somebody who is unlikely to drink or will make it harder for drinking to occur
⦿ if going out, only take a limited amount of money
⦿ if going out, do so at a different time of the day and/or week
⦿ if at home, change the environment (lighting, furniture)
⦿ if still drinking, change the drink or the people with whom drinking
⦿ keep only small amounts of alcohol at home

Developing a generic coping plan

When the client faces stressful situations, they are more likely to employ well-rehearsed and maladaptive coping strategies than newer and more adaptive ones. It is therefore important for the client to develop a generic coping plan that can be adapted to any major crisis. This could include:

⦿ a list of phone numbers of supportive and reliable others
⦿ a list of safe places where the client can ride out the crisis. It is crucial that such places have very few or no drinking cues
⦿ a flashcard (see the next therapy session for an example) that will include a set of positive thoughts that can be substituted for drink-related thoughts, a list of the negative consequences of using alcohol and a set of reliable distracters

Out-of-therapy session practice

The client should be asked what they think may be useful to implement from the session in avoiding or coping with stimulus conditions. Examples of what could be implemented include:

- keeping a diary of activating events (see example above) and identifying how these were coped with
- practising the strategies identified above and ones that will be covered in the next sections
- thinking about a stimulus condition that is likely to arise before the next session and, with the practitioner, write a plan of what is going to be done to avoid or cope with it. Out of session it will also be important to practise the response to the situation and note how the response worked out
- drawing up a generic coping plan

TACKLING CRAVING

Introduction

Craving can be described as a subjective sense of desiring to attain the state induced by using alcohol. This desire is typically a mixture of physical and emotional arousal, thoughts and memories. It is almost inevitable that when the client stops or reduces using alcohol they will experience craving, although its intensity and frequency will be subject to individual differences. Because craving is a potent trigger of alcohol use, it is important to target it early on in therapy by:

- educating the client about the phenomenon
- modifying uncontrollability beliefs and
- developing and enhancing skills to manage it

Craving as a phenomenon

It is important for the client to recognize that craving is common and normal, and can occur sometimes even after several years of abstinence. The experience and nature of craving can be verified through self-report: "Can you describe what it feels like for you to be craving alcohol?" and "How bothered are you by alcohol craving?" Another point that needs to be conveyed to the client is that craving frequency and intensity will abate over time the less it is acted upon (i.e. the less alcohol is used to control it). In addition, any episode of craving will abate naturally if unfulfilled. It is useful to think of craving simply as a signal to take action before a drinking episode ensues. The typical situations that may trigger craving will include:

The environment

Triggers associated with drinking are a major source of craving. These will include the sight of alcohol or a pub, seeing other people drink and time cues (e.g. a certain time of the day and/or a day in the week).

Memories of the drinking life

Sometimes a client will find themselves thinking of their drinking as a long-lost friend or partner and have thoughts such as: "A cold one really tasted good", "I remember how good it felt when I would drink a few on a lovely summer evening", "What's going out in the evening without a drink?"

Emotions

When experiencing both pleasant and unpleasant thoughts and feelings, or when bored or stressed, a client is more likely to experience craving. For example, when wishing to enhance a positive experience, a client may have learned to associate the relaxing effects of drinking with socializing and think that drinking will make social interactions more 'enjoyable' and 'spontaneous'.

Some clients are able to gain a better understanding of cravings by keeping a craving diary. This involves recording all the times that they experience a craving. If the client feels as if they are always craving, it is better to start with the times when the craving is at its worst or gets worse.

Modifying uncontrollability beliefs

A client with drinking problems will frequently report uncontrollability beliefs about their craving. Examples of these types of beliefs typically include:

"Craving is a physical reaction, so I cannot do anything about it."
"Craving will make me go crazy."
"I cannot control my craving."

Table 3.2 Evidence for and against the uncontrollability of craving

Craving belief	Strength of belief (0–100%)
(a) "Craving is a physical state, so I am powerless over it"	90%
(b) "When I am craving alcohol I cannot function and cope"	90%
Evidence for	**Evidence against**
Evidence for (a): At times I get a powerful and overwhelming craving for alcohol, and the only way to deal with it is to drink because it is the body needing the alcohol.	Evidence against (a): There are many reasons that can trigger craving that are to do with the environment and my mood rather than what my body feels like, which is a consequence of these. I've managed to control my craving in the past when I was not at home or when I was distracted.
Evidence for (b): I cannot seem to concentrate on anything when I am craving alcohol. It takes up all my resources.	Evidence against (b): At times, I have managed to go to work, be with friends and play sports when I was craving. This actually helped to deal with it and I found it would not last forever.

Outcome

With commitment and a vision for a better future, I can accept and control my craving. Experience suggests that it is not an entirely physical reaction but has much to do with where I am, what I am doing and what I am feeling. Craving does not last forever! The more attention I pay to it, the worse it becomes. I have resisted even severe craving. I can do it again. I know what to do. Craving now is infrequent and usually mild and short-lived. Such craving isn't a big problem.

Re-rating of belief in each thought (0–100%)

(a) "Craving is a physical reaction, so I cannot do anything about it" (10%)
(b) "When I am craving alcohol I cannot function" (10%)

There are good reasons why a client might hold these beliefs, not least because in the present and past they will have struggled with craving and/or ended up drinking to relieve it. However, these sets of beliefs are unlikely to be true all of the time, and will tend to engender rumination about one's own incompetence at controlling internal states such as craving. This, in turn, will increase the frequency and duration of negative emotion episodes associated with self-evaluation, which will act as further triggers for craving and alcohol use. The exercise presented in Table 3.2 is aimed at evaluating the evidence for and against the uncontrollability of craving.

It is important for the client to understand that at times they may be misinterpreting the evidence relevant to their craving. The questions they could ask themselves to challenge the evidence for lack of control over craving include:

"Is the evidence for lack of control over my craving true 100% of the time?"
"Is there evidence that it might not be true 100% of the time?"
"Do I really drink every time I have a craving?"
"Have there been times when I have not experienced craving in a craving-inducing situation?"
"Can I recall one episode when my craving stopped once it had started?"
"Have there been times when I could have given in to my craving and did not?"

Considering what the evidence suggests and writing a brief summary of the conclusions is crucial for the client to crystallize their appreciation of how thinking about craving can become distorted over time. At this stage the client will have probably realized that some of their uncontrollability beliefs about craving may not be completely grounded in evidence. Despite this, they may still doubt the fact that they can have some control over their craving. This is because they are likely to have reservations about the new belief that they can control their craving. These reservations are natural and are typically expressed in the form of the familiar "yes . . . but" sentences. A typical example would be: "Yes, I know I can control my craving but only when I am with people". Giving up beliefs about craving will not be easy for the client because their beliefs take responsibility away from them. Craving is perceived as something that takes over and cannot be controlled rather than something that can be directly controlled. A very important part of tackling craving successfully will be for the client to accept that they are responsible for what they do and that they can do things differently if they so wish.

Developing and enhancing strategies for managing craving

To begin with, it is important to know which strategies, if any, the client already uses for managing craving. Simply asking "Do you do anything to counter the experiences of craving?" may shed light on the nature of these strategies. The following is a suggested course of action that typically helps the client be prepared to manage craving. After outlining the key steps of action, it is useful to ask the client "What do you feel would work best for you?" This sub-topic can then be examined in further detail, possibly over several therapy sessions.

Relaxation

One of the first things the client should try to do when facing an episode of craving is to relax. Is the client familiar with relaxation strategies? If not, they may find it useful to learn brief relaxation strategies that only take a few seconds or minutes to perform (see page 106).

Positive self-statements

The presence of craving may make it difficult to reason objectively. Generating positive self-statements can be helpful to get through the initial critical period (15–20 minutes) of craving. The things that the client could say to themselves should not be over complicated and should primarily be a reminder of the positive things that are being attained by not using alcohol. It might be helpful for the client to remember the following:

⊙ to avoid statements with a punishing element to them
⊙ to say something to themselves that they believe in
⊙ if using phrases and statements feels false and unconvincing, then it may be better to use images of scenes or memories that are pleasant and personally relevant

The following are examples of positive self-statements:

"I will put up a fight."
"I'll feel healthy and remorse-free in the morning."
"I can spend money saved on gigs, CDs, visits or clothes."
"I'll be taking responsibility for myself and my future."

Distraction

Together with relaxation strategies and using positive self-statements, the client may need to employ strategies aimed at reducing the focus of attention on the craving experience. Whatever strategy is chosen needs to be mentally absorbing. Clients often report that physical activity is particularly useful for distracting oneself from craving. The activity should also be enjoyable and meaningful. In addition, it appears to help if the activity lasts for a reasonable period of time (e.g. more than half an hour). Strategies include:

⊙ describing surroundings (e.g. shop fronts, cars, monuments, people) and attempting to go into as much detail as possible with their descriptions

- ⊙ talking, which may involve a conversation with a friend, colleague or family member
- ⊙ removing oneself from cue-laden environments (e.g. a pub, people drinking) by, for example, taking a brisk walk, visiting a friend or going for a drive
- ⊙ household chores, which will not only serve as distraction but will also help to boost self-esteem because of accomplishing something useful
- ⊙ games (e.g. board games, video games, cards or puzzles) that can be quite challenging and require concentration

Image replacement

It is commonplace for a client, especially after a few weeks of abstinence or reduced drinking, to picture or dream about drinking. In these images, drinking is usually perceived as a method for coping with distress. It is helpful to substitute the positive image with a negative image regarding the damaging consequences of drinking. This may include feeling hopeless and anxious, losing money, jobs and partners. If this image replacement strategy causes distress, the client may want to replace the positive image of drinking with a positive image regarding the benefits of not drinking. This may include being back at work again, having more money, being able to take care of their children and so on.

Review the benefits of not drinking and the costs of drinking

Thoughts about the positive consequences of not drinking and the costs of drinking will weaken craving. The client should make their personal list of both from the material developed in the earlier sections.

Decisional delay

When having a craving episode, the client should introduce a rule of putting off the decision to drink for 20 minutes. Craving will usually go or subside substantially if no drink is taken during this period of time, and the client should be reminded of this.

Developing a flashcard

The client can sum up all the information on managing their craving on a flashcard. This will be invaluable when craving occurs and it needs to be tackled quickly and effectively. An example of a completed flashcard is shown in Figure 3.1.

Managing My Craving

Distraction: (a) describe surroundings; (b) phone a friend or boyfriend but don't talk about craving; (c) do chores; or (d) learn a poem.

Coping statements: "I'll feel healthy and remorse-free if I don't act on it"; "I can spend money saved on gigs, books or clothes"; "I'll not be creating financial, occupational, or emotional problems for myself"; I'll be breaking negative patterns of behaviour now rather than later, and be making life easier for myself"; and "I'll be taking responsibility for myself and my future".

Visual images: (a) replace a cosy drinking image with a drinking image that is negative (e.g. being somewhere or doing something I'll regret; nasty memory; head buried in the pillow; going to the off-license on Saturday afternoon; (b) an image of myself as strong, while crushing, in one hand, a glass of wine.

Figure 3.1 An example of a completed flashcard

Cue exposure and response prevention

Some CBT protocols, in line with a classical conditioning perspective, advocate managing craving through cue exposure and response prevention. This consists of repeatedly exposing the client to the sights and smells of alcohol without allowing the use of alcohol. This should be done until the craving elicited by these cues is substantially weakened or extinguished. In order to be able to expose the client to the relevant stimuli, a thorough assessment of cues and stimuli that elicit craving must be undertaken. This should result in a hierarchy of situations. Starting with the situation that evokes the least craving, the practitioner should expose the client to the situations from the hierarchy. The emphasis of this form of intervention is on external cues such as sights and smells or the locations (e.g. the pub) where the alcohol is used. Cue exposure and response prevention should be undertaken in vivo (that is, exposure to the real situation) but can also be accomplished by using imagery or watching videos of alcohol use. In all cases, not leaving the situation when feeling uncomfortable and not drinking (response prevention) is fundamental for habituation to take place. The subjective levels of craving and associated feelings should be assessed throughout the exposure sessions by having the client rate them on a scale from 0 (no craving) to 10 (extremely strong craving).

It is important to note that the more realistic the exposure, the more craving will be elicited, and – if successfully resisted – the better the outcome will be. When compared with therapy for anxiety disorders (such as phobias), where part of the therapy can be performed as an out-of-session assignment without supervision by the practitioner, such self-controlled exposure in vivo in problem drinkers is not recommended. It has also been suggested that a client can build further resilience to cues and contexts for alcohol use by exposing themselves also to internal cues for alcohol use, such as negative emotion. In a client whose craving is elicited by the latter, it is advisable to repeatedly expose them to those cues by negative mood induction. This can be done by imagery and mood induction procedures (listening to sad music).

Cue exposure and response prevention is a useful and theoretically sound strategy for weakening the link between external/internal cues and problem drinking, but at present should be considered as an add-on rather than a primary intervention. This means that if conducted properly, cue exposure and response prevention should be placed in the context of other important strategies (such as developing skills and attaining a balanced lifestyle) to ensure that the client is able to benefit from it fully.

Out-of-therapy session practice

The client should be asked what they might practise that will be helpful in managing craving. Examples include:

⊙ keeping a daily craving diary. (and adding a column for how they coped)
⊙ practising one of the strategies identified above
⊙ practising relaxation exercises
⊙ developing a flashcard

FOCUSING ON SKILLS

Introduction

Central to the CBT approach to problem drinking is overcoming skills deficits. A variety of strategies are used to help the client increase their skills in detecting and coping with high-risk situations that commonly precipitate alcohol use. The key areas to address are:

⊙ refusing drinks
⊙ receiving criticism about drinking
⊙ assertiveness

⊙ identifying apparently irrelevant decisions and
⊙ problem-solving

It is important to consider that a client may have been drinking for a long time and have never adequately developed or strengthened these skills or that they may possess adequate skills that have fallen into 'disuse'. For some clients, therefore, focusing on these skills will contain much that is novel; for many others, it will provide a needed review.

Refusing drinks

It is crucial to prepare the client for situations in which people around them will offer a drink or pressure them to drink. This is a high-risk situation to be in, especially for a client who has recently decided to stop or reduce their drinking. Family gatherings, office parties, dates, dinners with friends are some of the settings in which alcohol will be encountered. Fellow workers, relatives, dates might offer a drink without knowing the client's drinking history. This may range from a single casual offer of a drink to fully fledged urging. Being able to say "no" to a drink will require more than a simple commitment to stop drinking. Specific assertiveness skills are necessary. These will allow the client to respond more effectively to real situations when they arise.

Managing voice and eye contact
The client should aim to refuse a drink in an unhesitant manner. Their voice should be clear and firm. This should be done so as to prevent questioning about whether one means what one is saying. The client should also ensure that they make direct eye contact with the other person, as it will increase the effectiveness of the message.

Changing subject of conversation and suggesting an alternative
After refusing the drink, the client should change the subject of conversation so as to avoid being drawn into a debate about drinking. The client may also want to do something else, such as go for a walk or a drive, or suggest something else to drink or eat (coffee, dessert).

Asking for a change in behaviour
If the person continues to pressure the client, the client should clarify that they do not want to be offered a drink anymore. For example: "Thanks for offering me a drink one more time. I just don't want it, so stop asking me."

Avoiding excuses and vague answers
Phrases such as "I am not that well" or "I usually would have one, but not tonight" will only serve to postpone having to refuse a drink. The client should try not to provide excuses as this might also imply that at some later date they will accept the offer of a drink, putting more pressure on themselves and the person offering it. That said, in extreme cases excuses may be a last resort.

Rehearsing
The practitioner should rehearse with the client their drinking refusal skills ahead of encountering any high-risk situation. In the example below, a client prepared himself ahead of a wedding reception, where he knew he would inevitably be offered a drink.

Other (practitioner): Would you like a drink?
Client: I'll have a coke, please.
Other (practitioner): Come on. Just one drink! It is an important day! Don't spoil it by being boring!
Client: I'm not drinking at the moment.
Other (practitioner): Why not?
Client: Drinking doesn't agree with me.
Other (practitioner): Why doesn't it agree with you?
Client: There are plenty of other things we can talk about. Stop bothering me about whether I want to drink or not and let's talk about something else.

During a role-play it is important not only to rehearse the verbal component of refusing but also to pay attention to body language and behavioural expression of refusal.

Receiving criticism about drinking

In day-to-day life, a client is bound to stumble across critical statements. If criticism is delivered properly, it is likely to provide the client with a chance to learn valuable things about themselves and how they affect others. If it is not, it may lead to communication breakdown and arguments. The client's potential inability to respond effectively to criticism can trigger critical interpersonal conflicts, whereas an effective response can minimize conflicts, and consequently the probability of drinking. One of the most difficult things to achieve in exchanges with others is to learn to interpret any criticism received in a benign manner, ensuring that the focus is on separating personal emotions about the criticism from the information presented in the criticism. For many clients problematic drinking patterns may have affected their life in a variety of ways that makes them susceptible to criticisms about their behaviour. This is why it is especially important that the client is able to respond to criticism in a constructive way.

Criticism can be destructive or constructive. Neither warrants an emotional or hostile reaction. Destructive criticism arises when someone criticizes a person, rather than their behaviour. The intention of this form of criticism may be to hurt a person. This type of criticism is often linked to the other person's emotional state or may be a provocation to fight. The use of the words 'always' or 'never' features prominently in destructive criticism:

"You are always home late, you will never stop drinking!"

Constructive criticism targets behaviour and not the person. In this case the other person attempts to describe his/her feelings with regard to a given behaviour and usually asks for change in some way:

"I worry when you are late coming home. I start thinking you may be on a binge. Could you let me know you are ok?"

Criticism can also take many forms. A typical one regards slips ("Here we go again, you went out with Joe . . . you are drinking again!"). A client will often find that even if they are committed to stopping drinking, it may take time for others in their life to increase trust and to diminish their own excessive vigilance about reoccurrence of drinking episodes. Sometimes this criticism is unfounded, sometimes it may not be. In both cases it is important for the client to learn to respond in a way that fosters constructive communication rather than fighting. At times, criticism will focus on past drinking ("I hated you when you were drinking, you destroyed our family"). It is crucial for the client to avoid ruminating about the past and use their resources for focusing on here-and-now solutions. During the initial period of sobriety, criticism about drinking may be accompanied by criticisms about other behaviours the client may display or have displayed. For example, a partner may be upset about the client's low mood and desire to be alone. However, instead of directly addressing these behaviours, they may avoid mentioning them and focus instead on the present risk of drinking or past drinking behaviour. This unfounded criticism may occur because drinking has been associated with these other behaviours in the past (for example, a client may have started drinking when her mood was low), or because criticizing drinking has become an automatic process. Again, irrespective of how the criticism is phrased, it is fundamental for the client to be able to clarify the person's real concerns. This will not occur unless the client can respond adequately to the initial criticism, thus avoiding getting diverted into a fight or a discussion.

The following tips are aimed at improving the client's ability to receive criticism (irrespective of whether it is constructive or destructive) and to understand important information contained in the criticism.

Avoiding counterattack
Getting defensive and responding with criticisms will only fuel the argument, preventing effective communication from taking place.

Obtaining more information
Finding out more about the criticism in question will encourage straightforward statements about the client's behaviour, which are more likely to improve communication. For example, if a client's partner criticizes them wanting to spend time on a new hobby, a non-confrontational reply (uttered in a calm tone of voice) could be something on the lines of "I cannot figure out what it is about my hobby that aggravates you. Could you tell me?"

Agreeing and restating in a clearer manner
Instead of responding aggressively, a client can try to accept those negative things that are said about them that may, in part, be true. For example, if a client has not been drinking but a partner says:

"You are always home late, you will never stop drinking!"

A client may reply by saying:

"You are right; I almost always come home late. This has to do with my job, but I understand why you are concerned since when I used to drink I always used to be late too."

In this reply, the part of the initial statement that was right ("You are always late. . .") is validated. The part of the statement which relates to the partner's concern and is expressed destructively ("you will never stop drinking!") is restated. This takes away the negativity and confrontation element of the initial statement, allowing the partner to respond more objectively.

Compromising
This entails proposing some behavioural change as a response to the criticism. In the example above it may mean ensuring that some days during the week the client comes home early.

Assertiveness

A major issue for many problem drinkers lies in developing and using skills of assertiveness. Examples include being able to handle awkward social situations (for example, asking for directions or complaining to someone), dealing with confrontation and refusing reasonable requests without feeling overwhelmingly guilty or angry. Developing and/or strengthening assertiveness skills will provide an effective way for the client to let others know what is going on within, as well as what effect the behaviour of others has on the client. Being assertive frequently results in correcting a problem that is at the source of stress and tension. This stress and tension, if not dealt with properly, may lead to problematic drinking. Acting assertively will thus decrease the chances of the client using alcohol inappropriately as well as improve quality of life. Being assertive means being:

- able to recognize one's rights and the rights of others
- able to clearly state one's feelings and needs
- aware of what one wants and does not want and acting accordingly
- able to confront difficult situations head-on instead of being intimidated, afraid, aggressive or manipulative

An aggressive interpersonal style is characterized by:

- imposing one's needs and feelings on others
- running over others' rights while protecting one's own
- attempting to achieve one's goals even when others are hurt or treated unfairly

A passive interpersonal style is characterized by:

- failing to communicate one's needs and feelings
- giving up one's rights to avoid conflict
- always wanting to please others

Assertive people will occasionally act in a passive way (e.g. with an insensitive boss) and can also respond aggressively (e.g. with a pusher). However, by and large, assertive people are free to be who they are, and are more likely to have their needs met. They also tend to experience less interpersonal stress and have better social relationships. Learning how to assert oneself is an essential step in claiming personal happiness and well-being.

Enhancing assertiveness
Becoming more assertive involves a number of steps that the client will need to practise:

1 Thinking before speaking – The client will have to decide in advance what they want and what is fair. They will need to prepare themselves about their:
   a. request ("I want to discuss . . . with you")
   b. feelings ("I feel . . . about the situation")
   c. needs ("I would appreciate you doing . . . about this situation").
   It is important for the client to question their assumptions about other people's intentions. Are they being objective and rational? Discussing it with the practitioner is helpful if unsure. Writing things down also helps clarify thoughts. In addition, having a contingency plan for coping if things do not go smoothly is essential.
2 Asking for what one wants clearly – The client should attempt to be brief and specific, and avoid rumbling on the same point. Stating one's needs in a factual manner and waiting for a response. Avoiding side-tracking, and theorizing and practising how one is going to state one's needs beforehand is necessary.
3 Being aware of body language – Posture is important. The client should stand tall, respect personal space and maintain eye contact as it shows sincerity, confidence and interest. Fidgeting should be avoided. Facial expression and tone of voice should match the message being put across.
4 Listening to what the other person has to say about the request – the client should be sure to understand their point of view and ask for clarifications if they don't. Willingness to compromise is essential. Restating one's assertion if one feels not heard is also necessary.

Handling confrontation
Handling confrontation in an assertive manner involves solving a problem with another person whilst maintaining self-respect. The DESC (Describe, Express, Specify and Consequences; Broe, 1995) routine provides a useful way of remembering how to do this:

Describe – The client should attempt to make a factual and non-blaming statement of what has happened in an episode of confrontation. For example, "In the meeting you told me off in front of the team."
Express – The client should say what they felt. For example, "I was utterly angry with you and embarrassed by you."

Specify – The client should say exactly what they would like the other person to do. For example, "In future, if you want to criticize me, please do so with greater consideration. Remember other people were present."

Consequences – The client should say what will happen if both parties agree. For example, "If you do, I'll be able to engage better and feel less threatened and we will both be better off."

The process is one of negotiation. This means the client should:

- when appropriate be prepared to find a compromise that satisfies the needs of both individuals
- make sure that both people know exactly what has been agreed
- express appreciation of the other person's agreement to change, and eagerness to keep to what has been agreed and
- avoid trying to resolve additional issues until the present issue has been settled

The practitioner should role-play easy examples to begin with, and swap roles with the client. For example, the client could role-play taking a faulty product back to the shop where it was bought, and not wanting a replacement or a voucher, but simply a cash refund.

The DESC routine should be employed to get what the client wants without being aggressive and/or threatening. Additional strategies that could be used by the client include:

- broken record – repeating the main point in the same calm tone
- disagreeing – simply uttering the words "I don't agree"
- emphasizing emotions – repeating statements of how one feels and stating how important this is
- agreeing to disagree – recognizing the other person's point of view but repeating one's own
- redefining – not accepting the other person's labelling; restating one's positive opinion of one's actions
- questioning – not accepting vague criticisms; demanding clarification (e.g. "can you explain to me why exactly I got it wrong")

Common difficulties

Sometimes, a client will become very emotional about an issue, especially if they have not confronted it for some time or are confronting it for the first time. Nervousness, doubts and aggressiveness are likely to emerge. The client should try to remain calm by maintaining a relaxed posture, applying controlled breathing (see page 106) and stating their needs. Shifting attention to the other person and listening to what they have to say rather than keeping self-focused attention and scanning for signs of discomfort will also help. The practitioner and client should bear in mind that it is arduous to change one's interpersonal style and that it will take time and practice to do so. It can also be quite frightening to assert oneself, especially if one has adopted a passive style for a number of years. Trying to change things gradually is the best option. Again, as with other exercises, asking the client to make a list of things they would want to change and working from the bottom of the list, the easiest things first, will help to attain the overall goal of changing interpersonal communication style. Over time, self-efficacy will grow and the client will start reaping the benefits of being able to assert their rights and needs.

Identifying apparently irrelevant decisions

During the course of the day, a client will make numerous decisions that could potentially lead to alcohol use. Some of the smaller and more ordinary ones will appear to have nothing to do with drinking. In reality, it may be these smaller and more ordinary decisions that cumulatively lead a client to a point at which drinking becomes probable. It is hard to recognize for the client, when in the midst of the decision-making process, that they may be heading for a 'slip'. This is because so many choices do not appear to involve drinking at the time the client is considering them. Apparently irrelevant decisions refer to those rationalizations and minimizations of risk that may lead the client into drinking situations. They also refer to events that individually may appear unrelated but that together can lead to a high-risk situation. These are sometimes described as 'set-ups'. For the client, they can lead to alcohol use if not recognized and managed at an early stage. Each stage offers an opportunity for a choice to be made that may take the client away from, or towards, alcohol use. This topic is closely related to previous ones in which the client will learn how to identify and cope with stimulus conditions and craving. However, some of these situations may be hard to predict or difficult to avoid and in such cases the exercises that follow will help the client to identify the role of decisions made early in the chain that may lead to alcohol use.

One of the most effective things the client can do is to try to think about decisions they have to make that may lead to drinking. This will involve thinking ahead about possible options and anticipating high-risk situations. The first step is to identify an apparently irrelevant decision the client has made that resulted in using alcohol. The client should think of a time, in the recent past, when they had a slip after a period of abstinence. They should ask themselves the following questions:

Table 3.3 Decision sheet on past slips

Preceding event/situation	Apparently irrelevant decision	What could have been done differently?	Advantages of doing things differently	Disadvantages of doing things differently	Safe alternative
Early evening. Working poorly. Felt low and frustrated. Recently found out ex-boyfriend has new partner.	Aimlessly walking around town, on my own.	Engaged in an activity that would have given me pleasure (e.g. cinema, running) and felt I had some mastery of.	Would have taken mind off work and boyfriend, and improved my mood.		Visit cinema or go running.
Lying in bed during the day.	Visualized drink and elation experiences.	Get out of bed and replace positive drinking images with realistic images of its costs. Do something distracting (e.g. read a poem).	Would have taken my focus away from craving and reduced it.		Replace positive drinking images with realistic ones. Do something distracting (e.g. read a poem).

⊙ what events and/or situation preceded the slip?
⊙ who was I with?
⊙ where was I and what time of the day and week was it?
⊙ what decisions led to the slip?
⊙ what could have been done differently?
⊙ what are the advantages and disadvantages of doing things differently?
⊙ what will I do next time – what is the safe alternative?

Examples of apparently irrelevant decisions that may lead to a relapse can include: not making plans for the weekend, keeping alcohol at home, going to a party where people are drinking, and going to the pub to see old drinking pals.

The exercise presented in Table 3.3, the Decision Sheet on Past Slips, is aimed at evaluating the steps that have led to past slips and what could have been done differently. In addition, advantages and disadvantages of taking a different decision are evaluated. Once the client has completed this exercise, they should repeat it with any apparently irrelevant upcoming event that they think may lead to drinking. An example of this can be

Table 3.4 Decision sheet on upcoming events

Preceding event/ situation	Apparently irrelevant decision	What could be done differently?	Advantages of doing things differently	Disadvantages of doing things differently	Safe alternative
Jeremy invited me to his wedding reception on 24 April 2008	Accept invitation	Decline invitation	Avoid a risky situation	It wouldn't be nice to miss his wedding reception	Rehearse drinking refusal skills. Review motivation exercises, and leave early
Lisa and Joanne have asked me to go on holiday with them during the winter break	Accept offer	Decline offer	Avoid risky situation	Greatly disappoint my friends and lose an opportunity for a fun and relaxing time	Accept, but, prior to holiday, fortify myself (i.e. plan things to do on holiday, rehearse drinking refusal skills, and review my exercises)

found in Table 3.4. It is important to remember that decisions may involve any aspect of the client's life, such as friends, recreational activities, family or work. When faced with a high-risk option, the client should generally choose a safe alternative. On the other hand they may, for some reason, decide on a high-risk option. If they do so, the practitioner should help them to plan how to reduce their chances of drinking.

Problem-solving

Effective problem-solving necessitates the client recognizing that they are facing a problem situation and resisting the appeal of either doing nothing or responding precipitately. Generating an effective solution will require pausing to assess the situation in order to be able to decide which actions will be in one's interest. Not identifying a good solution to the problem will lead to its escalation. This may, in turn, act as a trigger for drinking. Problem-solving skills are thus a necessary component for tackling problem drinking effectively, since any problem can set the stage for a slip. Two common types of problem-solving deficits are:

1 not thinking through situations to evaluate alternatives and
2 thinking that one has good problem-solving skills, but reacting impulsively when confronted with a problem

Problem-solving skills are not specific to alcohol-related problems and should be developed and strengthened so that they can be applied to any problem encountered in life. Whatever the problem, it is beneficial to take a systematic, planned approach to dealing with it. The following tips (adapted from D'Zurilla & Goldfried, 1971) are aimed at improving the client's ability to deal with problems as they arise.

Recognizing the problem
The first and most important task for the client is to identify whether there is a problem to tackle. Some of the clues that usually indicate the presence of a problem include: physical sensations (craving, indigestion, palpitations), thoughts and feelings (particularly worry, but also anxiety, low mood, anger and many other emotions), behaviour (neglecting one's appearance, poor work performance) and interaction with people (being criticized).

To the client it may seem, at times, that there is no single problem but a myriad of them. Alternatively, a single problem may be identified but the client may feel it is impossible to solve it. Either way, the client will need to list the problems they have as specifically as possible. Once this is done, a hierarchy of problems can be set out in which it is worth tackling an easier problem first. More difficult problems can then appear increasingly solvable as self-efficacy in problem-solving improves.

Having recognized that something may be wrong, the client should attempt to define each problem as precisely as possible. This will entail gathering information and being concrete. Breaking down the problem into small parts will make it easier to manage each part rather than confronting the problem as a whole. For example, an imminent party might give rise to the following concern: "I have to attend Philippa's birthday party in a fortnight and be friendly with Caroline." This concern reflects two sub-problems:

1 "I have to deal with being anxious at meeting people and being offered a drink" and
2 "I have to see my ex-girlfriend Caroline and be polite to her"

Generating solutions
It is important for the client to generate a number of solutions to any given problem, because the first one that comes to mind may not be the most appropriate. Several approaches can help in this process:

⦿ Mindstorming – when the client mindstorms they should attempt to generate solutions without evaluating whether they are good or not. It is best that the client writes them down on a piece of paper as they come, so that they can be reconsidered once the process is over
⦿ Past solutions – the client may be able to think of a solution that worked before, or ask someone else about solutions that have worked for them in the past. It is likely that an 'old' solution will have to be 'tailored' to fit present needs
⦿ Reframing – it may be of help to take a step back from the situation. How would the client advise a friend if they had the same problem they did?

Solutions to "I have to attend Philippa's birthday party in a fortnight" may include:

⦿ send my apologies
⦿ have a drink in order to calm down
⦿ recall how I coped in previous and similar situations and
⦿ talk about the concerns with a friend

Evaluating the advantages and disadvantages of the solutions

Once the client has generated solutions, they will need to evaluate the advantages and disadvantages of each in order to decide which will have to be rejected because of its unsuitability. For example:

⦿ send my apologies: reject, as it is Philippa's 40th birthday
⦿ have a drink in order to calm down: reject, as I am not drinking now
⦿ recall how I coped last time: accept, as I did quite well at a party a week ago and successfully refused drinks that I was offered
⦿ talk about my anxiety with a friend: accept, as some of my friends can be supportive

Choosing a solution

Following this, the client will have to rank the solutions according to their usefulness at the present time:

1st solution: recall how I coped last time
2nd solution: talk about my anxiety with a friend

Planning to implement the solution

Once the client has done this, they should take their first choice solution and start planning how to put it into action, ensuring the following questions are addressed:

⦿ what will I do?
⦿ how will I do it?
⦿ when will it be done?

⊙ who will be involved?
⊙ what is my back-up plan?

The problem-solving action would entail:

⊙ finding a place where the client will not be disturbed
⊙ recalling all the details of the previous party and writing down all the strategies the client remembers helped get them through the evening
⊙ if not able to remember, try the 2nd solution

Whenever possible, the client should try to rehearse dealing with the problem (in this example, going to the birthday party) either by imagining it or by role playing with the practitioner or someone they know.

Implementing the solution and evaluating performance
Implementing a solution and reviewing whether it is successful or not is crucial in completing the problem-solving process. If successful, the client should congratulate him or herself and remember what they did for future occurrences. If unsuccessful, the client should try to understand what went wrong. Perhaps that particular day they were not feeling great, or may have been over-ambitious or have misjudged elements of the problem. Obstacles should be reviewed with the practitioner so as to learn as much as possible from the experience.

Planning for future problems
Finally, the client should be reminded that not all problems can be anticipated. Enabling the client to think ahead about forthcoming situations that could be problematic (as is done in tackling apparently irrelevant decisions, for example) and working through them using problem-solving skills is a good exercise to be undertaken.

Out-of-therapy session practice

The client should be asked to practise skills regularly, ensuring that they do not set themselves up for a situation they cannot handle. Practising assertiveness skills may involve making one reasonable request per day (e.g. asking for directions) and ensuring the client records the situations (how they felt and what happened as a consequence of asking). Other activities may include practising saying "no" to requests where the client wants to say "no" but does not feel like doing so.

In terms of apparently irrelevant decisions, the client should self-monitor decisions over the course of several days and identify safer versus riskier decisions. With respect to problem-solving, the client should again monitor the problems they encounter and note how they respond. A further exercise would entail asking the client to choose an example each day of a simple problem and to write their problem-solving process in the manner identified earlier.

MODIFYING BELIEFS

Introduction

Beliefs are cognitive structures that are not easily modified by experience. In CBT it is generally maintained that there are three key types of beliefs that are relevant to problem drinking: positive or anticipatory beliefs/positive outcome expectancies, permissive or permissive beliefs, and uncontrollability or impaired control beliefs.

Positive beliefs are important because they can help trigger drinking episodes. They constitute learned information about an association between events. This information is understood to be of an 'if–then' nature; if a certain event is presented, then a certain event is expected to follow. Examples include:

"Drinking makes me more affectionate."
"Drinking reduces my anxious feelings."
"Drinking makes me more sociable."

Permissive beliefs (also known as 'rationalising') typically involve themes of entitlement, minimization of aversive consequences and justification. Such beliefs are thought to undermine an individual's ability to tolerate craving and will fuel a drinking episode once it has started. Examples of these types of beliefs include:

"I will just have one more drink."
"Another drink won't harm me."
"Now that I have started drinking, I might as well carry on."

Uncontrollability beliefs relate to self-perceptions regarding the inability to control drinking. These beliefs are thought to play a central role in lapsing and relapsing because they are associated with escalations in negative emotions/perceptions of the self, which can trigger alcohol use. Examples include:

"I have no control over my drinking."
"I cannot stop myself."
"My drinking persists no matter what I do."

Identifying beliefs

In order to modify beliefs related to problem drinking, it is important to identify which are crucial for the individual client. Identifying these beliefs is accomplished through:

⦿ functional analyses of drinking episodes and
⦿ exercises aimed at identifying and challenging beliefs

It is crucial to learn to identify beliefs 'on-line' (i.e. as they are occurring). However, doing this is not straightforward and a client will need to practise spotting beliefs as they become activated in different situations (e.g. before, during and after a drinking episode). The exercise in Table 3.5 is aimed at identifying permissive beliefs. This exercise also can be applied to positive beliefs (see Appendix M). Activating events for positive beliefs typically include stimulus conditions as identified through functional analyses and other exercises. Activating events for uncontrollability beliefs tend to be related to emotional and physiological (e.g. hangover) states that follow a drinking episode. The restructuring of uncontrollability beliefs is presented in page 88 'Drinking postponement experiment'.

Examining and challenging beliefs

Beliefs usually develop over an extended period of time. As a result they become entrenched. Given the rigid nature of beliefs, the process of modifying them is usually an arduous task. After the practitioner has identified the client's key beliefs, the examination and challenge of these beliefs should begin.

Examining beliefs

The process of guided discovery (or Socratic Method) should be used at this juncture. This method is based on active questioning and selective

Table 3.5 Identifying permissive beliefs

Activating event	Feelings and sensations	Permissive beliefs
On a Thursday, I was on a solo walk along the river in Fulham. I passed a few pubs and off-licences and experienced a strong desire to drink. I stopped and had one.	Bored, frustrated, and worried. Slightly elated from the possibility of having a drink.	"I've only got £40 so I can't do too much damage." "I can start afresh Monday."
During my slip period, on one occasion, I went into a pub with the intention of drinking no more than two pints of beer. I drank four.	As above.	"I've got to drink more." "Another few drinks won't do any harm."
When did it happen? Where were you? What were you doing? What were you thinking about?	What feelings and body sensations did you notice?	What were you saying to yourself that made it easier to keep drinking? Highlight the key belief that makes it most likely for you to continue drinking.

NB. In the case of uncontrollability beliefs, the last column would include prompts such as "What were you saying to yourself that made it more likely to start drinking again?" and "Highlight the key belief that makes it most likely for your drinking to start again"

reflection occurring in a non-judgemental atmosphere. It allows the client to develop an awareness of their own beliefs and associated behaviours. This method should be balanced by clarification, feedback and education based on what is being discussed. Questions should be phrased in a manner that engenders self-awareness rather than requiring a correct answer. The principles of collaborative empiricism are adhered to by asking for evidence in support of or against a particular belief, seeking alternative explanations, questioning the range of consequences of a specific belief, and evaluating the impact upon the individual of changing their beliefs. The following dialogue between practitioner and client illustrates this process.

Practitioner: Let's look at your beliefs about drinking.
Client: Well, it's been over two weeks since I had a drink. Long time. . .
Practitioner: Do you miss it?
Client: Yes, in all honesty; a lot.

Practitioner: What do you miss specifically?

Client: The good feeling, the friends, being with people.

Practitioner: So, drinking is fun and it makes you relax.

Client: That's right. What can be better than being at the pub with your mates and having a good time?

Practitioner: So you don't think that there is anything as much fun or as relaxing as having a drink with your mates?

Client: Well . . . not really.

Practitioner: Are you sure?

Client: Well . . . yes!

Practitioner: Ok. Let's look at that belief in more detail. Firstly, how confident are you that there is absolutely nothing as much fun as a drinking session with your mates?

Client: Well maybe there is, but I am not aware of it.

Practitioner: You started drinking heavily in your mid to late 20s. Prior to that, what would you have done for fun? We are talking about 25–30 years, of which maybe 10 years you must have spent doing something else to enjoy yourself.

Client: Well, I remember being bored and anxious in social situations. Bored with my job and life as a whole. Nervous, at times, with people around me. Yes, definitely.

Practitioner: So perhaps you initially turned to drinking to deal with boredom and the monotony of your life?

Client: Yes.

Practitioner: It must have been a difficult time in your life.

Client: Yes, definitely.

Practitioner: I guess drinking may have provided a simple and instant solution to the problem. What do you think?

Client: Thinking about, I mean, thinking about it in more detail, maybe yes.

Practitioner: Maybe?

Client: More than maybe.

Practitioner: Returning to your original belief: "Nothing is as much fun or relaxing than drinking". When you began drinking heavily, had you explored other options to deal with monotony and anxiety?

Client: Not really. Drinking was there. At an arm's length.

Practitioner: So what evidence do you have that drinking is really the only option for fun and relaxation you can have with your mates?

Client: If you put it this way, and looking back at how it all started, I think I got into drinking at a time in my life when anything that took me away from being bored and anxious would have been good.

At the beginning of this dialogue, the client was confident that nothing was as rewarding as drinking. However, through the practitioner's questioning, the client began reconsidering the belief. As the strength of the belief waned, the client could begin replacing the maladaptive belief with a more adaptive view of their behaviour.

Challenging beliefs

Continuing with the example of permissive beliefs, once the key beliefs have been identified, there are questions the practitioner should ask that will be useful in challenging these beliefs:

⊙ do these beliefs make it easier or harder to drink?
⊙ what would you say to someone else?
⊙ what are the consequences of thinking in this way?
⊙ what could you say to yourself that would make it easier to stop drinking?
⊙ what would someone else say about these beliefs?
⊙ is this situation similar to past situations?

The Socratic Method provides the first step towards examining and, to a degree, challenging beliefs. However, to cement gains further it is important to consider evidence against beliefs as well as to develop and strengthen more adaptive and alternative beliefs. It is crucial to do this in written form as it will allow the client ready access to data on their beliefs in circumstances when they may need it most (e.g. following a slip or when a trigger for drinking is presented). The exercise can be extended to include additional columns used for challenging beliefs. In this way the client can have an overview of the process ranging from activating events and associated beliefs to evidence not supporting the beliefs and alternative beliefs that can be constructed. An example of a completed exercise with permissive beliefs can be found in Table 3.6.

It is important for the client to challenge beliefs as often as possible. The client should also ensure that they keep records of the work they have done with them at all times. If they do drink, they should record and challenge their beliefs as soon as possible. If the client engages in this exercise on a regular basis they should find that maladaptive beliefs will start weakening and that adaptive beliefs will start developing and strengthening. This, in turn, is likely to decrease the chances of a drinking episode occurring or to limit a drinking episode once it has started.

The client should not become dejected if progress is not swift and should be advised not to expect to achieve too much too soon. It takes time to generate alternative beliefs, especially when the client may be challenging a variety at the same time.

Practising the activation of adaptive beliefs

On completing the guided discovery and belief restructuring exercises the client will be far more attentive to the disadvantages of drinking. It is also

Table 3.6 Challenging permissive beliefs

Activating event	Feelings and sensations	Permissive beliefs	Evidence not supporting the beliefs	Alternative beliefs	Strength of alternative beliefs
On a Thursday, I was on a solo walk along the river in Fulham. I passed a few pubs and off-licences and experienced a strong desire to drink. I stopped and had one.	Bored, frustrated, and worried. Slightly elated from the possibility of having a drink.	"I've only got £40 so I can't do too much damage." "I can start afresh tomorrow."	I have borrowed money from flatmates or friends before. During my 10-week slip period, I had this thought many times, and yet I found it extremely difficult to stop.	"I can borrow money; and even if I only spent £40, I'd be strengthening a tendency to drink when feeling bad or bored." "Past experience tells me that I'm unlikely to be able to 'start afresh on Monday'. It isn't that easy."	90% 90%
When did it happen? Where were you? What were you doing? What were you thinking about?	What feelings and body sensations did you notice?	What were you saying to yourself that made it easier to keep drinking? Highlight the key belief that makes it most likely to continue drinking.	Use the six questions provided to challenge your belief.	Note the alternative more helpful belief.	Rate the strength of your belief on a scale from 0 to 100%.

likely that the client will have developed adaptive and alternative beliefs to strengthen resolve against future problem drinking behaviour. However, it is likely that the client will not be able to readily access these new beliefs in the presence of powerful triggers as they will be relatively 'under learned' compared with maladaptive ones. Hence the practitioner needs to pay attention to the activation of adaptive beliefs through two methods:

1 the development of flashcards (as in tackling craving) and
2 programmed practice

Items that could be included on a flashcard might be:

"Using alcohol is fun, but it will eventually kill me."
"When I use alcohol I become increasingly dependent on it."
"Drinking is relaxing, but has many disadvantages."

Programmed practice (or covert rehearsal) is done in therapy sessions via imagery. The client is encouraged to imagine an event that evokes craving. As the craving increases, the client is asked to activate adaptive beliefs in the therapy session in order to control the craving. The following dialogue between practitioner and client illustrates this process.

Practitioner: You said earlier that it was easy to ignore your newly formed beliefs when you are tempted by alcohol. Today I would like you to practise activating adaptive beliefs so that they can come more naturally to you when you find yourself in tempting situations.
Client: Ok. I think it makes sense, since when presented with those situations the older beliefs are really prominent.
Practitioner: I would like you to imagine and describe a situation in which you are tempted to drink. Be as detailed and vivid as possible in your imagination and description. When this is done properly it is common to start craving alcohol. This is what we are looking for, because when it happens we will practise activating your control beliefs.
Client: Ok. I see where you are coming from. A bit concerning however . . . I am home alone, having returned from work. I come in through the front door. Same pattern, I sit on the sofa in the sitting room and turn on the TV. Thoughts come to my mind: "I am stupid", "I am a parasite". Anyway, I start feeling very low. I can feel things caving in around me. I want to cry. I look through the door to the kitchen. I can see the fridge. Same door, same handle. I think: "Have one", "You will change tomorrow", "It will release you." I just get up and like a robot I head for the fridge. It is all automatic, exciting. I am going to get it now . . . (attention returns to the practitioner) . . . you've managed to make me crave it. What am I going to do now?

Practitioner: Is the craving present and strong?
Client: Yes, pretty much so.
Practitioner: Fine. Start reviewing your control beliefs out loud.
Client: The disadvantages of using alcohol?
Practitioner: Yes. Take out the flashcard if you want.
Client: "Using alcohol is fun, but it will eventually kill me", "When I use alcohol I become increasingly dependent on it", "Drinking is relaxing, but has many disadvantages". Drinking is killing me! It makes my life miserable. I can let it go if I want to.
Practitioner: How are you feeling now?
Client: I can make it!

In this dialogue the client managed to recreate a craving to use alcohol but successfully countered it by activating adaptive beliefs. This process should be repeated several times over a few therapy sessions.

Drinking postponement experiment

For a client who is higher on self-efficacy or who has a greater degree of control over their drinking behaviour, a behavioural experiment can be carried out to test beliefs about the uncontrollability of alcohol use, such as "I have control over my drinking".

Every drinking problem is different, so the client will need to design and carry out the experiment that will work for them. It is also crucial to ensure that the experiment is graded, starting from a situation in which the client thinks it will be relatively straightforward to confirm they have control, and gradually build up to the more difficult situations. Hopefully, over time, the client will be able to tackle the most difficult situations. This type of intervention is similar to cue exposure and response prevention, but differs in three ways:

1 the exposure may not be as specific (smelling alcohol)
2 response prevention is limited to not drinking and the client can leave the situation when they like and
3 the exposure is explicitly linked to the confirmation and disconfirmation of beliefs

The experiment suggested is the drinking postponement experiment. A client begins by identifying all the situations in which they find it difficult not to drink. They make a list of these situations and then rate each situation on a scale from 0 to 100%, with 0 being 'not at all difficult' and 100 being 'extremely difficult'. Once this is done, the situations are

Table 3.7 Hierarchy of difficult situations

Situation	Difficulty (0–100%)
Being home alone	100%
Walking past the pub on the way home	90%
Walking past the corner shop on the way home	80%
Feeling upset or bored	75%

ranked in ascending order of difficulty. A sample hierarchy of difficult situations is presented in Table 3.7.

Once the client has finished this exercise they will be ready to carry out the experiment. Table 3.8 presents data from a completed experiment. Before undertaking the experiment, the client should begin by writing, in their own words, the belief (in the example this is ''I will always end up drinking if prompted'') they are going to test at the top of the worksheet, and then rate it on a 0 to 100% scale. The client should then write what they plan to do in the left-hand column under the heading 'Experiment to test belief'. In order to increase the probability of success, the client should ensure that they think about possible problems (as in the apparently irrelevant decision exercises) and how they plan to deal with them (if they do occur) under the heading 'Strategies to deal with problems'. The client should then carry out the drinking postponement experiment. When they have done this, they should record both the date and details of the outcome and re-rate their belief on a 0–100% scale. Once this is done, they can consider repeating the procedure for the next most difficult situation. This exercise should be continued until the top of the client's list is reached. This whole process may take a few weeks, and it should be borne in mind that only practice will help the client attain long-term changes in maladaptive beliefs.

Out-of-therapy session practice

The client should be asked to apply adaptive beliefs in real-life situations through the postponement of drinking experiment. Testing beliefs to evaluate their validity is also useful. For example, a client may be challenged to try various methods for having fun or relaxing in order to test beliefs such as ''there is nothing more fun or relaxing than using alcohol''.

Table 3.8 Drinking postponement experiment

Before experiment			After experiment	
Belief to be tested and strength (0–100%) "I will always end up drinking if prompted" – 80%			Belief to be tested and strength (0–100%) "I will always end up drinking if prompted" – 40%	
Experiment to test belief	Possible problems	Strategies to deal with problems	Date of experiment	Experiment outcome
To walk past the pub on the way home and not go inside for at least a week. Every day I've been going in for the last month after work.	I might meet a friend who will ask me to go for a drink.	Say no.	The week commencing 23 September.	The strategies were of great help.
				I only met once a guy I usually drink with and told him I was not up for it.
	I will crave a drink.	I will wait and see if the craving goes away.		A few times I had a strong craving but waited for it to go away and went for a long walk.
	There might be a football game on and I will want to see it.	Go in to see it and focus on the match rather than drinking. Refuse drinks if offered.		I did go to see a game and did just that. I drank a can of coke.
				The thought that my drinking is uncontrollable is not always true – I seem to have a choice and ways of doing things that can actually help me to control it!

MANAGING NEGATIVE EMOTION

Introduction

There are multiple sources of negative emotion in clients presenting with problem drinking. Comorbidity and co-occurrence with other mental health problems is elevated, and anxiety and mood disorders are quite common. Rates of sexual and physical abuse are also high, and the consequences of these problems often include a component of strong negative emotion. Intense negative emotion that is associated with another mental health problem should be treated in line with the appropriate protocols (see page 118 'Addressing complicating problems').

Dealing with negative emotion that is not associated with a mental health problem presents a series of challenges. For example, when a client first reduces or stops drinking they may experience a wide spectrum of emotions as unfamiliar and intense. These emotions may be linked to craving, withdrawal or simply having limited experience of coping with the emotional variation that is part of everyday life. Understanding the link between negative emotion and drinking is the first step in learning how to manage drinking. This should be followed by implementing coping strategies aimed at dealing with negative emotion. These may include: increasing pleasurable activities, tackling boredom, restructuring cognitions, dealing with anger, interrupting recyclical thinking, improving sleep and relaxation.

Psycho-education

The practitioner should begin by describing negative emotion and how prevalent it is in problem drinking. For example:

"Research shows that many people who experience problems with alcohol also experience problems with anxiety and low mood. By anxiety I mean a negative state usually characterized by bodily symptoms of physical tension and apprehension about the future. Depending on the situation, you can also call this experience 'fear' and 'worry'. By low mood I mean a state in which one repeatedly thinks about negative themes, feels the need for reassurance, broods about unpleasant events and feels pessimistic about the future. One may feel hopeless, guilty, unmotivated and completely uninterested in what usually are pleasurable activities. Ultimately, however, these are just labels for something that feels bad, uncontrollable and is unwanted."

Following this, an overview of how alcohol may have been used to cope with negative emotion should be outlined. For example:

"Many of those who suffer from problem drinking have a history of anxiety and low mood before they became problem drinkers. It is thus reasonable to view prolonged and excessive alcohol use as a learned way to cope with underlying negative emotion. The difficulty with using alcohol as a coping strategy is that its effect on negative emotion is very temporary and becomes increasingly so the more one becomes dependent on alcohol. By using alcohol to control, regulate or avoid negative emotion, i.e. to stop experiencing the dread, fear, negative thoughts, worry, bodily sensations, low mood or whatever form it may take, we mistakenly teach ourselves (i.e. learn) that negative emotion is only controllable by using alcohol."

Finally, the key idea that the client's negative emotion can be managed should be presented:

"Nobody escapes negative emotion as it is an integral part of life to experience it. Negative emotion can become a problem when it is exaggerated and when a cycle of distress develops that is managed through alcohol use. You can learn to break this cycle and deal with negative emotion by modifying your thinking style and widening your coping strategies."

Key strategies

Some of the strategies that the client will have already implemented (e.g. dealing with stimulus conditions, tackling craving, modifying beliefs) may have brought about a significant improvement in negative emotion. Conversely they may have exposed the client to experiencing greater levels of negative emotion, especially in those clients in whom using alcohol was the primary tool for regulating emotion. It is thus advisable to implement the strategies presented as early as possible in therapy.

Increasing pleasurable activities

One of the most common concerns a client will have is that stopping drinking or changing one's drinking patterns will expose an empty life. This may well be the case if the client has had a life composed of little beyond eating, sleeping and drinking. In this case, giving up drinking would entail giving up a large chunk of recreation time, social activities, friends and past ways of having fun. In other words, key sources of pleasure. The absence of these sources of pleasure will make negative emotion a more prominent feature of the client's emotional landscape which, in turn, will increase the chances of wanting the quick fix of a drink. This is why it is of paramount importance for the client to engage in pleasurable activities when they stop or reduce drinking, as these will

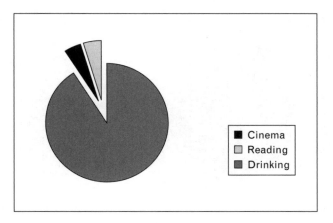

Figure 3.2 Sources of pleasure when drinking is a central activity

lead to an improvement in mood and a reduction in the probability of slipping. A series of steps can be followed in helping the client increase pleasurable activities in their life.

Step 1 – Reviewing existing sources of pleasure
Scheduling pleasurable activities is one of the most powerful interventions to improve mood and simultaneously inhibit the client's desire for drinking. To begin with, however, it may be useful to review existing sources of pleasure by breaking them down and presenting them to the client in pie chart form, as shown in Figure 3.2. Following this, it is important to highlight how little would be left that would generate pleasure if drinking were to stop, as shown in Figure 3.3.

This exercise will help the client gain an initial understanding of how limited the repertoire of their pleasurable activities is likely to be, and how important it is to develop a portfolio of pleasurable activities to compensate for the loss of pleasure derived from drinking and associated activities.

Step 2 – Learning to monitor pleasurable activities
A crucial second step is to get more accurate information on the client's current levels of pleasurable activities by monitoring them. This can done quite easily by keeping a record of activities during the week and rating how much pleasure the client derives from them and how good they think they are at these activities (mastery). The Activity Diary in Table 3.9 is an example of a record for logging activity patterns that will help the client structure their record keeping. This diary was completed at the

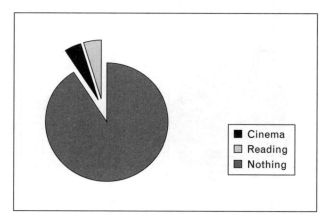

Figure 3.3 Sources of pleasure when drinking alcohol ceases

beginning of therapy. It is clear the client was spending much of the week sleeping and getting little pleasure out of anything except being with his friends in drinking situations and reading. When completing their diary, the client should ensure that they state the activity they are engaged in, and the levels of pleasure and mastery it gives them on a scale of 0 to 10 (where 0 is little pleasure and 10 is a lot of pleasure). It is important that the client fills their diary on regular basis.

Step 3 – Developing a list of pleasurable activities
Once the client has collected accurate information on what they are doing during the week, what pleasure they are obtaining from the activities and their level of mastery, it is possible to begin listing pleasurable activities that the client would like to initiate or increase in frequency. Some of these pleasurable activities may well be things the client used to take pleasure in but has not done in a long time. Others may be things they have wanted to do but never got round to trying. William Glasser (1985) argued that pleasurable activities can become 'positive addictions'. A negative addiction, such as alcohol, can be described as an activity that feels rewarding at first but eventually becomes undesirable and detrimental. A positive addiction (e.g. swimming) is an activity that may not be instantaneously rewarding but usually becomes increasingly desirable and beneficial in the longer term. An activity that is positively addictive meets the following criteria:

⊙ it does not necessarily depend on others
⊙ it is non-competitive

Table 3.9 Activity diary

Week: 5/5/01	Monday	Tuesday	Wednesday	Thursday	Friday	Saturday	Sunday
9–10	Asleep	Asleep	Asleep	Asleep	Asleep	Asleep	Asleep
10–11	Asleep	Asleep	Asleep	Asleep	Asleep	Asleep	Asleep
11–12	Asleep	Asleep	Asleep	Asleep	Eating P9/M5	Asleep	Asleep
12–1	Asleep	Asleep	Asleep	Asleep	Eating P9/M6	Reading P9/M6	Asleep
1–2	Asleep	Asleep	Eating P6/M4	Asleep		Watching TV P5/M5	Asleep
2–3	Asleep	Watching TV P4/M3	Watching TV P1/M1	Eating P8/M5		Watching TV P5/M3	Asleep
3–4	Asleep	Watching TV P1/M1	Watching TV P1/M1	Shopping P6/M4		Watching TV P3/M2	Asleep
4–5	Reading P7/M5	Shopping P8/M4	Watching TV P1/M1	Shopping P7/M5		Watching TV P2/M2	Dozed P2/M0
5–6	Reading P7/M5	Watching TV P1/M1	Watching TV P1/M1	Eating P3/M3		At the pub P7/M6	Asleep
6–7	Reading P7/M5	Watching TV P1/M1	Watching TV P1/M1	Eating P3/M3		At the pub P8/M6	Asleep
7–12	Tidying flat P5/M6	Watching TV P1/M1	Eating P9/M6	Watching TV P9/M4		At the pub P9/M6	Watching TV P1/M1

P = Pleasure (from 0 to 10); M = Mastery (from 0 to 10).

⊙ it has some personal value and
⊙ it can be improved with practice (but the client is the only one who is aware of their progress)

It is also important to ensure that any activity chosen has a balance between pleasure and mastery. Choosing activities that are too demanding, though pleasurable, may engender feelings of failure in the client. Conversely, choosing activities the client perceives to have high levels of mastery in, but are not very pleasurable, is likely to engender boredom. Both these emotional states can easily act as triggers for alcohol use.

Examples of pleasurable activities include exercise (swimming, cycling, jogging), hobbies, reading, relaxation, cultural pursuits and creative skills (art, writing, music). The client should be asked to generate a list of things they have been doing and would like to do more of, and things they have never done that they would like to do. Physical exercise is probably the single most important activity to engage in, as it almost always helps the client to redefine himself as healthy and physically fit causing cognitive dissonance and increasing motivation for change. It also helps to break recyclical thinking patterns (rumination and worry) and most importantly leads to a release of endorphins and an associated sense of well-being. Physical exercise should be graded, taking into consideration the client's level of fitness and medical condition. Medical advice should be sought if appropriate.

Step 4 – Developing a pleasurable activities schedule
Once the client has completed a list of pleasurable activities, they can start scheduling a small block of time each day (30–60 minutes) devoted to them. The goal is to gradually increase the activity levels and to maximize pleasure. The client can begin this process by taking some time to sit quietly and mentally review their list of pleasurable activities. They will probably not want to do the same thing every day. One day, for example, they may feel the need for exercise, another day for a hobby, and yet another day for relaxation. It is advisable to schedule some time each day, but not schedule the activity, so the pleasurable activity does not become an obligation. When the client feels that they have achieved consistency in the small block of time each day (30–60 minutes), they can gradually increase to a more substantial block of time (60–120 minutes). The practitioner has to remind the client to keep their activities in manageable proportions and to define their personal success realistically. It is also important to stress to the client that putting a pleasurable activity schedule into action requires commitment. They must be prepared to

establish priorities and possibly rearrange other activities in their life. The goal is to achieve an adequate balance between the activities they should do (eating, sleeping, working) and the activities they want to do (i.e. pleasurable ones). This is why scheduling is fundamental, as is ensuring the client can anticipate what problems or circumstances will interfere with their plans and they will take care of them.

A few tips should be followed to make the pleasurable activities schedule a help rather than a hindrance:

- being flexible – the client should remind himself that events may happen to throw him off schedule. These events should not be reason to give up
- thinking of alternatives – some of the activities scheduled may not be accomplishable because of factors outside the client's control (e.g. a friend not turning up for a dancing session, transport problems). An alternative should always considered
- following the schedule – there may be occasions when the client is unable to accomplish what they have planned because of sudden and competing demands (e.g. wanting to clear up the house and ending up talking to a neighbour). In these instances the client should progress to the next activity and plan to accomplish the task on another day. If another activity is finished sooner than planned, the activity which was missed may be undertaken

Step 5 – Comparing activity diaries
Once the client has a completed list of pleasurable activities, and has scheduled and engaged in pleasurable activities for a period of 4–6 weeks, it is advisable to review progress by comparing the initial Activity Diary with the most current and recent ones. Even if small differences are noticeable, this will provide impetus for engaging in further activities as well as strengthen self-efficacy. It is also useful to quantify changes that may have occurred. For example, how much more average pleasure the client gets presently compared with at the beginning of therapy, or the reduction (e.g. in hours) of an unwanted activity such as watching TV or oversleeping. Hopefully the client will see that there is a general trend towards increasing pleasure that goes hand in hand with an improvement in mood.

Tackling boredom

Irrespective of the pleasurable activities scheduled and their achievement, boredom will feature prominently in clients who have given up drinking. This is because life is not exclusively made up of pleasurable activities and engaging in these activities alone will not suffice in compensating for boredom. Becoming generally more active (sorting out bills, doing housework, etc.) is a powerful way to overcome boredom; however, when faced with something the client is willing to accomplish they may well experience thoughts such as "I will not enjoy it" or "It is boring". These thoughts are likely to inhibit action. The following are strategies that can be used for tackling boredom and increasing the chances of engaging in purposeful activity.

Carrying out practical tasks

Inactivity and boredom will often lead to procrastinating in undertaking practical tasks. The accomplishment of these tasks can be as rewarding as engaging in pleasurable activities. This point should be put across to the client. The client should also be asked to do the following:

1 make a list of everything that has been put off
2 rank the tasks in order of priority, or if these tasks are too burdensome, to accomplish relative to the client's present capabilities, in order of achievability (from the easiest to the hardest to achieve)
3 take the first task and break it down into small units
4 rehearse the task and think of practical difficulties that may be encountered
5 note any negative thoughts that arise from thinking of doing the task
6 begin the task in a step-by-step fashion, running through the small units identified and dealing with negative thoughts and practical difficulties as they arise
7 as soon as the task is finished, note what was done in the activity diary and rate it in terms of pleasure
8 note down thoughts on what it means to achieve the task
9 begin the next task and follow the same steps

Removing thought blocks

A powerful way to overcome inactivity and associated boredom is to identify and challenge negative thoughts that may act as blocks for progress. The practitioner should give examples of such thoughts together with possible answers to them, emphasizing that these are not the right answers but just answers, and that with practice the client will be able to find their own. The strategies for challenging these thoughts will entail using the Socratic Method and rationalizing strategies described earlier. Examples of typical thoughts and possible answers include:

Automatic thought	Possible answer
"There is far too much to accomplish."	"Writing down what I have to do will make things seem less overwhelming. Things can be done in small steps."
"I don't want to do it."	"Whether I want to do it or not is irrelevant. I know it is just better for me to do it."
"I will wait to feel in the right mood to do it."	"There is never a right mood to do it in. Doing it will make me feel better."

Reframing the meaning of boredom

The idea that constant stimulation is necessary should be challenged through the use of the Socratic Method and cost-benefit analysis. The client will have to evaluate whether it is possible to be constantly stimulated and if so, whether it is a desirable goal to have. Re-framing boredom and developing ways of accepting it is also important. Empty time could be perceived as an essential experience for replenishing both mental and physical resources, for example. Behavioural experiments aimed at testing out the effects of tolerating boredom could be devised.

Restructuring cognitions

Frequently negative emotion results from assuming a negative thinking style about events that could straightforwardly be interpreted as positive or neutral. We thus tend to assume situations or events make us feel bad, when, in most cases, our thoughts about these events determine how we feel. The chain linking events, thoughts, emotions and behaviours can be summarized as follows:

Activating event ⟶ Thoughts ⟶ Emotions ⟶ Behaviour

| Negative thoughts | Negative | Unhelpful |
| Positive thoughts | Positive | Helpful |

The client should be probed to identify examples, from their own life, that can illustrate this chain of events. Typically clients will find this hard to do, arguing that negative emotions lead to unhelpful behaviour directly. However, it should be stressed to the client that frequently thoughts 'bridge' activating events and negative emotions and that changing thinking patterns is likely to gradually improve mood. An example of a negative emotion chain could be:

Activating event ⟶ Thoughts ⟶ Emotions ⟶ Behaviour

Partner was   "She wants to   Sadness   Drink
not friendly   leave me"

There are several things clients can do to restructure their thoughts. The first step is to learn to spot negative thinking. What kinds of negative thinking habits have become automatic for the client? The client should consider thoughts that might be linked to some negative emotion or activating event. They can begin with the following examples:

Activating event	Thoughts	Emotion
A work colleague was unfriendly	. . . .	Tension
	. . . .	
	. . . .	
Somebody says you are no good	. . . .	Depression
	. . . .	Anxiety
	. . . .	

Ellis (1975) has put forward types of thoughts that may not be helpful. The practitioner should probe the client in attempting to recognize any of them in their repertoire of thoughts. These include:

- self-put-downs – "I am pathetic"; "I am worthless"
- expecting the worst – "It will never work"; "All my relationships are doomed"
- unrealistic goals – "I must do everything right"; "Other people should always be reliable"
- catastrophizing – "If things do not go my way it will be the end of the world"
- black-and-white thinking – "If I am not completely loved all the time then it must mean I am loathed"
- overgeneralization – "I am always going to be nervous"; "I will never be on time"

Stopping these thoughts and replacing them with more neutral and constructive ones will help the client to experience less negative emotion. The practitioner can give an example of this process, such as a work colleague calling the client a "waste of space". In response to this the client could:

- let this depress them, which will mean that they are thinking something on the lines of: "Yes, he's right, I am no good", or
- let this anger them, which will mean that they are thinking something on the lines of: "How dare he say something like this about me?", or
- challenge the negative thinking with more positive thoughts, which may literally 'produce' a better mood, such as: "Maybe he has had a row with his partner and feels like taking it out on somebody. I know my worth and if I am a waste of space so is he! If I did do something wrong, I will put it right"

When reviewing scenarios that may trigger negative emotion, the client should be probed as to whether there are different ways to interpret situations, events and people's comments. They should also try to replace negative thoughts with more positive ones. The following are some strategies that can help 'neutralize' negative thinking patterns:

⊙ decatastrophizing – many times negative emotions arise from predicting catastrophic consequences. These thoughts can be challenged by examining the probability of feared events actually happening and the client's ability to prevent them from occurring
⊙ recalling positive things about yourself – for example, asking the client to remind himself of things that they usually do well. What good things have others said about the client or done for them?
⊙ challenging extreme thinking – thoughts that have 'shoulds', 'musts' and 'oughts' signal extreme thinking. For example, contrast with the client the thought: "My partner should love me for everything I do" with "It is nice if my partner wholeheartedly loves me, but he does not have to like everything I do"
⊙ mindfulness – the client should be probed to become aware of their thoughts and how they are linked to their negative emotions in a detached/observational manner. The client should also learn to tell themselves that anxiety, depression and anger are all signals that thoughts and actions may need constructive change
⊙ self-reward – if the client manages to handle a difficult situation well they should reward themselves. For example: "I began by being upset that I was not invited to a friend's party, but I did a good job at recalling positive things about myself and challenging my extreme thinking"

Dealing with anger

Anger is a common human emotion. It tends to occur when we are not getting what we want and when things seem out of control. It is usually the consequences of anger (such as aggression, passivity and impulsive behaviours) that increase the likelihood of drinking. This is why it is important to learn to cope with anger and upset in a constructive way. As with other types of emotions, addressing activating events and thoughts will help to control anger. Anger does not just occur randomly. Many clients will think that it is events or situations that make them angry, but in actual fact it is the thoughts about these situations and events that result in anger. The following are tips that will make anger more manageable:

⊙ identifying activating events – the first step in helping the client to manage their anger is to get them to become conscious of their activating events. What is it that triggers their anger? Is it the frustration of not achieving a goal, a verbal insult, an obscene gesture, seeing someone else being attacked?
⊙ writing down anger-inducing thoughts – the client should gradually become aware of the thoughts associated with anger. As explained in the previous section, any thought that is linked to an emotional reaction is likely to occur quickly and automatically. This is why the client will have to practise spotting their 'bridging thoughts' to anger. An example of this is presented below:

Activating event ⬜⬜⬜⟩ Thoughts ⬜⬜⬜⟩ Emotions ⬜⬜⬜⟩ Behaviour

| Someone jumps the queue | "How dare she!" | Fury | Shouting |

Can the client remember some thoughts that might be linked to episodes of anger in his life? The practitioner can begin with the following examples:

Activating event	**Thoughts**	**Emotion**
A driver cuts in front of you	. . . .	Irritation
	. . . .	
Somebody tells you you are an idiot	. . . .	Annoyance
	. . . .	

⊙ changing thoughts about the activating event – the client should try to keep calm by saying to themselves "relax" or "take it easy". They should begin by questioning their interpretation of the situation. Are they overreacting? Is it that bad? Are there any other more constructive thoughts that could help them feel less angry? The client can remind himself about the negative consequences of getting angry (e.g. drinking), and replace the negative thoughts with more positive ones. Examples could include: "Life is too short to get pissed off about anything"; "He is not really trying to hurt me, he is just upset about something"

⊙ changing behaviour in response to the activating event – implementing behaviours that will make the client feel calmer or help them solve the problem. These will include: asserting oneself to request change, leaving the situation, and talking to the person in a slow and rational way

There are going to be times when the client will simply not be able to resolve the situation and will still feel angry. It is important that the client understands that ruminating (brooding) about the event will simply increase upset. Engaging in a pleasurable activity, trying to distract oneself, or calling a friend to talk about it will help.

Interrupting recyclical thinking

Recyclical thinking includes rumination and worry. Both are styles of coping with negative emotion. Rumination is characterized by elevated levels of self-focused attention and persistent brooding about the past. Worry is characterized by perseverative mental problem-solving aimed at anticipating future events. Both these types of recyclical thinking have been shown to be an important factor in vulnerability processes leading to the occurrence of, and relapse into, dysphoria, major depressive disorder and generalized anxiety disorder.

A degree of recyclical thinking can be helpful if it is self-limiting and aids problem-solving, allowing the client to cope effectively with challenging situations. Here is an example of adaptive worry:

Frank has an interview for a job he really wants. He is worried about the outcome. He decided to prepare really well: he researched the company, prepared answers to the possible questions, organized a mock interview with his friend, and planned in advance what he is going to wear on the day.

Recyclical thinking can be classed as unhealthy if:

⊙ it becomes all-consuming
⊙ it feels uncontrollable
⊙ it is perceived as magnifying underlying negative emotion and
⊙ it is characterized by the recurrent asking of "Why did this happen to me" (rumination) or "What if X happens?" (worry)

Here is an example of unhealthy worry:

Frank constantly worries about the outcome of the interview. He fears that the panel of interviewers will not find him good enough for the job. In fact, he believes he will not be offered a job. This will be catastrophic as he is already in debt for his rent. These thoughts upset him so much that he cannot sleep at night. As a result, he is tired and cannot concentrate on anything. He finds waiting for the interview nerve-wracking. As a result, he has hardly prepared for the interview.

Unhealthy worry (as in the example above), as well as unhealthy rumination, limit the capacity to plan effective solutions to problems. In addition, by locking the client into virtual scenarios that are not amenable to disconfirmation, they exacerbate negative emotion, increasing the probability of using alcohol as a self-regulation strategy.

Strategies
Here are some strategies that will make the client's ruminative and worry routines more manageable:

⊙ turning rumination and worry into problem-solving – when the client 'catches' herself going down the recyclical thinking route, she should remind herself of problem-solving. The question to ask is: "What can I do to solve this problem?"

- writing down the content of rumination and worry – the simple act of writing down the content of recyclical thinking will make it less overwhelming
- mindstorming for solutions – making a list of possible things that the client could do to improve their situation
- evaluating each solution – how realistic is it? Can the client do it? What would it involve? What are the advantages and disadvantages?
- opting for the most realistic solution – deciding on the best possible (i.e. realistic) solution and working out the steps necessary to put it into action

If the client finds out that there is really no solution to the rumination or worry as it is completely outside of their control, then it is a signal that recyclical thinking is useless. Still, it may be difficult to switch off one's mind once recyclical thinking has started, so a postponement exercise can be undertaken.

Postponement of recyclical thinking exercise
The client should allocate some time each day to ruminate and/or worry. For example, 30 minutes in the evening each day could be scheduled in the client's diary as their 'worry time'. During this time, thoughts and worries should be allowed to roam freely. If a thought occurs during the day that is likely to ignite recyclical thinking, the client should note it down and remind themselves that they will think about it during their 'rumination/worry time'. Soon, the client will realize that many thoughts that may have triggered rumination or worry were actually not worth elaborating upon.

Improving sleep

The ability to sleep well should come naturally to us. However, it has been estimated that about 25% of people are troubled by frequent insomnia. An even greater percentage of sleep disturbances can be found in people with drinking problems. If the experience of sleep is exasperating, if sleep is not soothing, if a large part of the time is spent in bed distressed because one cannot sleep, then a large proportion of one's personal life may well be unpleasant.

If drinking is the cause of the client's sleep problems or is contributing to them, they will have to learn how to sleep without using alcohol. Establishing healthy sleep habits without alcohol will increase their confidence about being able to control their drinking. Many people find that alcohol appears to help them get to sleep. Indeed, anything that induces relaxation will be helpful in stimulating sleep. The problem is that alcohol's effects go beyond inducing relaxation. Alcohol is a drug that interferes with the normal sleep cycle. If during sleep one has alcohol in their bloodstream they may well end up not getting enough of the deepest (and most restful) kind of sleep. In addition, alcohol appears to increase the chances that a person will be agitated during sleep and will wake up more frequently during the night.

Not everyone who drinks experiences these effects, but in general one could argue that although alcohol may help in falling asleep, it will tend to cause marked sleep disturbances. It is also worth noting that when a person has become accustomed to alcohol and then decreases it or stops drinking, insomnia frequently occurs as part of the withdrawal from alcohol. If the client is not aware of what is happening, they may be tempted to utilize alcohol again to get to sleep. This will only make the problem worse.

Falling asleep is a completely natural process. It is not something that one has to learn or re-learn how to do. The natural progression from tiredness is to fall asleep unless there are obstacles that interfere with this process. Coping with insomnia, thus, is more a question of removing obstacles than of learning how to fall asleep. Things the client can do include:

- relax – the relaxation skills described later in this section will be helpful. Once the client relaxes physically, they may fall asleep naturally. The target is to focus on relaxing one's body and mind, not to make one go to sleep. Practising relaxation only at bedtime has its drawbacks, however, as the client may unintentionally learn to feel sleepy whenever they relax. This may not be desirable. The client should start by doing relaxation exercises at one other time during the day as well, when they are not getting ready to go to sleep
- select a regular bedtime and waking time – this is necessary because the body works best when it operates on predictable phases of activity and rest. It may also be helpful for the client to plan daily activities so that they begin to slow down as bedtime approaches. It is best to avoid spending the hour before bedtime in pursuits that require thorough planning, as this will usually escalate thoughts or worries
- avoid using the bed for anything except sleeping – some people are perfectly capable of reading or watching TV in bed and then quickly falling asleep, and for them it is no problem. If the client is lying awake in bed trying desperately to get to sleep, it is better to get up, leave the bedroom, and do something else. An option is to choose a length of time that seems reasonable to get to sleep. Probably this should not be shorter than 10 minutes or longer than 20–25 minutes. If the client has not fallen asleep during this amount of time, they should get up and out of bed and go to do something else until feeling sleepy. When starting to feel sleepy, the client should go immediately back to bed, practise relaxation, and allow himself to fall asleep
- avoid drinking anything containing caffeine within a few hours of bedtime
- avoid drinking alcohol within two hours of bedtime

- avoid drinking fluids just before going to bed to avoid waking up to go to the bathroom
- avoid smoking or using other drugs within two hours of bedtime
- avoid exercising within three hours of bedtime
- avoid having snacks if waking up in the middle of the night. The client may learn to feel hungry in the middle of the night, and hunger can wake them up
- improve the sleep environment by increasing comfort, reducing noise, darkening the room and having a good room temperature

It is worth reminding the client that awakening in the middle of the night and not being able to get back to sleep is to an extent perfectly normal. The body cycles through several stages of deep and light sleep, and sometimes in light sleep one awakens briefly. This seems to increase as people age. Awakening does not mean staying awake. Some sleep problems will require more extensive therapy and professional help. If the client has tried relaxation for a few weeks, along with the other strategies mentioned in this section, without improvement in their insomnia, they may want to seek additional help.

Relaxation

As discussed earlier, negative emotion can be a powerful trigger for drinking. In particular, anxiety can cause muscular tension, which in turn can give rise to a range of unpleasant physical sensations that can act as a trigger for drinking. These unpleasant physical sensations can be controlled by learning and practising a series of relaxation exercises. Over time the client should become proficient at responding to physical tension by using these exercises, which in turn will promote mental tranquillity and reduce the risk of drinking. Some of these exercises are outlined below.

Controlled breathing

Breathing is an automatic bodily activity that is performed without much conscious awareness. At times of physical exertion and stress we tend to breathe rapidly and in a shallow way. This rapid breathing has a function: we take more oxygen into our bloodstream, which makes it easier for us to sustain physical exertion (such as running away). It is a normal response to demanding situations, and when performed over short periods of time is not a problem.

Rapid breathing, also known as over breathing or hyperventilation, can become a problem when it lasts for long periods of time. This is because rapid breathing causes too much oxygen to enter our bloodstream, leading to numerous unpleasant bodily sensations: dizziness, visual problems, exhaustion, chest and stomach pains. All these can be quite frightening and can lead to escalations in anxiety and more rapid breathing, which in turn can result, occasionally, in a full-blown panic attack.

Controlled breathing is a strategy that can help to normalize breathing patterns at times of stress and anxiety. Breathing exercises have been found to be effective in reducing panic attacks, depression, irritability, muscle tension, headache and fatigue. The following steps can be used with the client to introduce controlled breathing:

Step 1 – Sit or lay down. If you are sitting, make sure your back is straight. Place your palms on your belly. Place the tip of your tongue against the roof of your mouth and keep it there throughout the exercise.
Step 2 – Inhale slowly (to a mental count of four) and quietly through your nose. Let the breath travel through to your belly. You will notice your belly rising underneath your palms.
Step 3 – Hold your breath for a mental count of five.
Step 4 – Exhale slowly through your mouth, making a whoosh sound to a count of eight. Pause.
Step 5 – Repeat. Take eight to twelve of these relaxing sighs and let yourself experience the feeling of relaxation.

Progressive muscular relaxation (PMR)
PMR was developed by Edmund Jacobson (Gessel, 1989). The PMR programme involves alternately tensing and relaxing different muscle groups in the body, which leads to deep relaxation. This strategy is based on the premise that the body responds to stressful events and thoughts with muscle tension. This bodily tension increases the subjective experience of anxiety and stress. So it follows that with deep muscular relaxation the bodily tension is reduced, which in turn leads to a decrease in subjective feelings of anxiety and stress.

Scientific research has shown that PMR is beneficial in the therapy of muscular tension, anxiety, insomnia, depression, irritable bowel syndrome, fatigue, muscle spasms, high blood pressure, neck and back pain, mild phobias, stress and stuttering. Running through a PMR session takes around 15 minutes. The following steps can be used with the client to introduce PMR:

Step 1 – Find a quiet place. It may help if you turn out the lights or draw the curtains. Try to minimize noise. The fewer distractions you have, the easier it will be to concentrate. A moderate room temperature and comfortable clothing may help as well. It is better if you are neither full nor hungry when you begin.

Step 2 – Make yourself comfortable. Sit or lie down comfortably, close your eyes and take a few deep breaths.

Step 3 – Practise the basic movement: tense and relax. Starting with your feet, tense your muscles by pulling the toes upwards. Do not strain, and concentrate on the sensation of tension. Hold for about five seconds and then release quickly and relax for 10 to 15 seconds. Observe how your muscles feel when you relax them. Repeat.

Progress in turn with different body parts. If there is a particular body part where you feel more tension, repeat the basic movement for longer.

Legs – straighten your legs, point your toes upwards, tense and hold for five seconds. Relax, let your legs go limp. Repeat.

Buttocks and thighs – squeeze, hold for five seconds and release. Repeat.

Abdomen – squeeze your abdominal muscles tightly against your spine. Hold and then release. Repeat.

Back – arch your back. Feel the tension and hold. Release and repeat.

Arms – stretch out your arms and hands. Clench your fists and hold. Release, let your arms and hands go limp. Repeat.

Shoulders/neck – lift your shoulders up and draw them as close as you can. Press your head back. Release and repeat.

Face – tense your forehead and jaw. Close your eyes and squeeze. Bite hard. Release. Drop your jaw and slightly open your mouth. Repeat.

Whole body – Tense your entire body. Hold the tension for a few seconds and then release rapidly. Repeat a few times.

Step 4 – Focus on your breath. When you have finished the practice, take a few deep breaths. Place your hands on your belly and observe the rhythmical movement. Spend a few minutes doing so. Get up slowly and move gently.

The client may want to start with an evening session first to help them unwind after work for example, and then build in a morning session as well. Once the strategy is mastered, a shorter version can be practised, which may involve tensing and relaxing the entire body or those body parts that feel particularly tense. Or simply omit the 'tense' stage and relax different muscle groups in the sequence.

Brief relaxation

The Brief Relaxation Procedure (BRP) was developed by Herbert Benson (1975). He wanted to help cardiac patients reduce the stress which worsened their condition. This simple relaxation procedure has since been established as very effective for reducing the symptoms of stress and stress-related illnesses.

As its name suggests, BRP is brief and can be practised anywhere: during a lunch or tea break for example, whilst waiting in a traffic jam, on the tube or bus: the opportunities are plentiful. A variant of this relaxation procedure is presented below.

Step 1 – Think of an image that you find calming. The image could be of a beach on a sunny summer day, a garden or a view from a mountain. In fact, it could be anything personally relevant or meaningful to you that brings sensations of calmness.

Step 2 – Sit comfortably. It may help if you turn out the lights or draw the curtains. Try to minimize noise. The fewer distractions you have, the easier it will be to concentrate.

Step 3 – Close your eyes. Imagine your body growing heavier and heavier. Feel the warmth from within your body and let yourself feel relaxed.

Step 4 – Breathe slowly. Breathe through your nose, and as you exhale think of the chosen image. Hold the image in your mind. Breathe regularly.

Step 5 – Keep going for as long as it takes you to feel relaxed. Your mind may wander off to the events of the day, or a worry that you have. Do not dwell on them. Do not try not thinking of them. Just accept them as thoughts and draw your attention back to your chosen image and to your breathing.

Meditation

Scientific studies have shown various benefits of regular meditation: boosting of the immune system that enables the person to better fight off disease, numerous changes in brain functioning that lead to a decrease in stress responses, and increased contentment and happiness (Kabat-Zinn, Lipworth, & Burney, 1985; Lazar et al., 2000). More and more medical doctors recommend meditation to reduce the negative effects of stress and anxiety. Meditation may prevent or at least aid control of the pain of chronic problems like cancer, heart conditions and AIDS. Even a 10-minute daily session can bring about dramatic effects. There are hundreds of meditation strategies. The client may want to search for the one that will feel right for them. Here is an example of a quick meditation.

Step 1 – Find a quiet place. It may help if you turn out the lights or draw the curtains. Try to minimize noise. The fewer distractions you have, the easier it will be to concentrate. A moderate room temperature and comfortable clothing may help as well. It is better if you are not hungry or full when you begin.

Step 2 – Sit comfortably. Sit in a chair, on the floor, wherever you find it comfortable. Rest your hands in your lap. Keep your back straight without tightness, and the chin pulled in a little.

Step 3 – Close your eyes. By closing your eyes you will be able to shut out the external world.

Step 4 – Focus on your breath, a word or phrase. Draw your attention to your breathing: to inhaling and exhaling and the rhythmical movement of your chest. Breathe slowly and regularly. Spend a few minutes doing so. Find a word or a simple phrase that means something to you, which has a soothing effect. If nothing comes to your mind say "om", "calm" or "love". Try saying your word or phrase to yourself with every out breath. Say it again and again.

Step 5 – Accept intrusions. You will notice that your mind will wander off to the events of the day, or a worry that you have. Some thoughts may pop up in your head out of the blue. Do not worry or dwell on them. Do not try not thinking of them. Just accept them as thoughts and draw your attention back to your word/phrase and to your breathing. Continue meditative practice for 10 minutes, or as long as you feel that you need to.

Maintaining change

WORKING WITH SIGNIFICANT OTHERS

Introduction

The involvement of significant others (a partner, friend and/or family members) can help in tackling problem drinking in several ways; for example, by providing positive responses to drinking abstinence, decreasing cues for drinking, giving support for not drinking, changing the nature of a relationship, and aiding access to further and new social support systems. The practitioner should thus consider involving a significant other in therapy. There are numerous ways in which this can be achieved, as presented below.

Responses to abstinence and drinking

Establishing or accessing a network of individuals who will provide differential reinforcement that is contingent on abstinence can be very helpful to a problem drinker. This reinforcement can be very straightforward, such as positive comments and encouragement or having a firm rule of 'no drink in the house'. It can also involve the negotiation of detailed contracts that specify the consequences of abstinence and drinking.

The 'community reinforcement approach' (CRA; Smith & Meyers, 1995) is aimed at helping the client access potential reinforcers (jobs, social clubs, training), enhancing motivation, teaching coping skills and developing contracts to make reinforcers contingent on abstinence. Compliance is typically monitored by a significant other. In addition to the manipulation of environmental contingencies, interventions may also focus on educating significant others about the importance of ensuring that the client learns to be exposed to and tolerate the naturally occurring consequences of drinking. This may well entail gradually making the client responsible as significant others frequently, and inadvertently, attempt to protect problem drinkers from these consequences (e.g. doing their chores, covering for them at work). The experiencing of these consequences is likely to increase the client's awareness of the extent and severity of the drinking problem and provide further motivation for change.

Decreasing cues for drinking

Significant others can inadvertently engage in a number of behaviours that may increase cues for drinking. A husband who wants his wife to stop drinking may repeatedly nag her about the problems caused by drinking, in the hope that his concerns will motivate change. Or a wife may try to get her husband to reduce his drinking by attempting to control his behaviour through limiting access to alcohol or keeping a tight control over money. Such behaviours can frequently have unintended negative effects, eliciting anger, arguments and tension. This, in turn, is likely to lead to further drinking. Significant others will need to learn to spot such behaviours and interactional patterns and acknowledge the negative results arising from them. Learning alternative ways to discuss concerns about drinking may be helpful in aiding the problem drinker.

Support for not drinking

Significant others can provide invaluable support by helping with the implementation of behaviour changes, discussing cravings, assisting in planning to avoid high-risk situations for drinking, and in the general implementation of other cognitive and behavioural strategies and skills presented in this book.

Relationship change

People develop basic beliefs about relationships and interaction styles early on in life from parents, peers, early dating experiences, media and society at large. These unrealistic expectations about relationships can limit satisfaction and promote maladaptive responses. A variety of CBT interventions can be employed to improve communication in relationships. These will include modifying unrealistic expectations, correcting faulty attributions in interactions and using self-instructional procedures. Dattilo (2002) provides an excellent introduction to this area.

Accessing and enhancing social support systems

Some clients will have either no social support systems or one that strongly supports drinking. In such cases, it is important to gain access to new systems that can reinforce abstinence or that may prove incompatible with problem drinking. Self-help groups can be a source of such support, as are group activities such as walking, running, cycling or hiking. Unfortunately, alcohol use can be an integral part of almost any activity. This is why it is important to review carefully any activity group and establish whether the group norm includes drinking. The client should follow three important steps when seeking new social support systems:

1 Reflect on the kind of support that is needed – this may include help with problem-solving, resources, information or emergencies. It could range from information on flats to rent or small loans, to jobs, local clubs and community activities.
2 Identify who might be of help – friends with similar experiences, people who are important in the client's life and can support their commitment to change. Family members are some of the most commonly sought people for help.
3 Think of how to get the help needed – strong relationships will take time and effort for the client to build, but some skills may be of particular help in this pursuit. Examples include:
   a Active listening – the client should be reminded of the importance of paying attention to advice. This will entail rehearsing social skills, such as keeping appropriate eye contact, showing interest and sincerity, respecting personal space, not interrupting, asking questions for clarification and paraphrasing what is heard to ensure understanding.
   b Provision of feedback – people that the client thinks will be of help will need guidance about what is and is not useful in their efforts to help. It is important for the client to acknowledge and thank them, as this will maximize the chances of receiving more help in the future.
   c Supporting others – a relationship where both parties help each other will be more reliable and satisfying than one in which a person always gives whilst receiving nothing. Helping someone out will not only benefit the recipient but also strengthen the client's coping skills.
   d Being specific – whichever form of help the client is looking for, they should be as specific and direct as possible in their request. This will increase the probability that they will get the help they wish and need.

If the client finds it difficult to develop social support systems, they may wish to consult an organization that can offer extra support (such as Alcoholics Anonymous or SMART Recovery) or seek specific treatment in the form of social behaviour and network therapy for example (Copello et al., 2009).

CONTINGENCY MANAGEMENT

Introduction

Contingency management (Higgins et al., 2003; Miller, 1975) is based on operant conditioning principles. In this type of intervention the environment is arranged in such a manner whereby reinforcement or punishment is contingent on alcohol use and associated behaviours (e.g. medication compliance). The aim of contingency management is to facilitate change in behaviour by providing attainable and clear goals for the client.

Principles of contingency management

There is no specific model of contingency management but rather general principles to guide its application in therapy. These are:

- regularity of assessment to verify that the client is adhering to the intervention programme
- agreement that rewards will not be provided if the client fails to follow the intervention programme
- collaboration towards the design and development of suitable alternative activities to drinking for the client
- consistency and immediacy in the administration and withholding of rewards

Typologies of reward that are most suitable to the client should be explored in detail so that a realistic and achievable system can be introduced. If significant others are involved in the implementation of the programme, they must have a full understanding of how it works. A reward should be given consistently and immediately on successful completion of a task. Examples of reward tasks include: attendance and useful contributions to therapy sessions, effort displayed in organizing matters that would arise on completion of therapy (e.g. education, housing, personal relationships, work). Rewards typically include vouchers for books, cinema, clothes, food and transport. Rewards should be increased over the course of time in line with the number of consecutive successful tasks accomplished. If the client fails to accomplish a task then the reinforcement schedule must be reset. Over time, and following continued success, the reinforcement schedule can be phased out. The following is an example of how contingency management can be introduced to a client:

"In addition to your therapy, you will be given the opportunity to earn what we call 'vouchers'. These have a monetary value. You will be able to earn them every time you achieve a task we have agreed upon. The vouchers can be used in whatever way we agree will support the lifestyle changes we discussed. For example, many people use their vouchers to buy books, go to the cinema or buy food. You will not receive cash directly, but all you need to do is decide with me the items you would like to spend your vouchers on".

The goal of contingency management is not only to reinforce abstinence from alcohol use but also to increase pleasurable activities that are alcohol-free, thus reducing the chances of lapses and relapses.

Difficulties with contingency management

A number of difficulties can arise when implementing contingency management. These typically emanate from a lack of careful planning and full understanding of the principles of operant conditioning. Some common difficulties that have been identified include:

⊙ rewarding only one behaviour – this will reduce the opportunities for generalization of adaptive behaviours
⊙ developing a reward schedule that will not work for the client – rewards need to be attractive enough for the client to want to receive them and simultaneously not too costly to the service
⊙ making this intervention central to therapy – contingency management may be useful in the early stages of therapy, especially as a means of maintaining motivation. However, it is not advisable to make this intervention a permanent feature of therapy as it will make the client dependent on it. The medium- to longer-term goal should be for the client to make decisions about using alcohol without relying on reward systems that cannot be part of everyday life

CONTROLLED DRINKING

Introduction

There is still controversy surrounding the issue of whether or not controlled drinking is a viable therapeutic goal. The orientation of this book is that it is a viable goal if a client wishes it to be, even if the only outcome is to demonstrate to the client that it was an unrealistic goal. Controlled drinking is likely to be a difficult goal to pursue. If the client has used alcohol in an uncontrolled fashion, over a long period of time, learning or re-learning how to drink in a controlled way will entail applying basic skills that may not be familiar to them anymore. A client deciding to pursue controlled drinking will therefore need to be committed to:

- carefully monitoring their drinking to be clear they are keeping to prearranged limits
- knowing what these limits are and
- utilizing strategies that will mean that renegotiating these limits will be more difficult (e.g. taking little money, telling drinking companions what the limit is)

A cornerstone of successful controlled drinking entails reviewing in great detail the times, places and cues responsible for activating drinking patterns and ensuring that the client is fully aware of these. It is also important to review with the client the solidity of their coping skills (in particular, assertiveness and problem-solving skills). Another important factor that needs to be discussed in detail is that of slowing down drinking. An agreement on the speed of drinking needs to be outlined (for example, one unit an hour). The client also needs to become fully aware that it takes some time for alcohol to bring to bear its effects. This is why, if the client drinks fast, they may well be feeling the second drink while they are having their third or fourth. This point has to be put across to the client clearly. In addition, it is important to highlight beliefs that may have developed about needing three or four drinks to get the effect desired when in reality this is not the case. A further important reason for the client to slow down, which should again be highlighted, is to ensure they can adjust their tolerance to alcohol. The more tolerant the client is, the larger doses of alcohol they will need to experience the same effect. Alcohol tolerance adjusts in relation to what is drunk, so as the client cuts back on their drinking their tolerance decreases. Some of the key controlled drinking skills that clients may find useful are outlined in Table 4.1 and an example of a brief controlled drinking programme is given in Table 4.2.

If a client fails to adhere to their controlled drinking programme, they will need a contingency plan. The practitioner should ensure there is support available in the form of a significant other, and that they are aware of the signs and symptoms of excessive alcohol use and have access to an emergency phone number and hospital in the event that these are observed. If the client does not have a clear contingency plan in place it is advisable to avoid attempting controlled drinking.

In conclusion, it is important to bear in mind that controlled drinking is more difficult than abstaining, as the latter entails just avoiding drinking alcohol. Controlled drinking, however, is open to deliberate or accidental miscalculation on how much the client may have drunk. In addition, both

Table 4.1 Controlled drinking skills (adapted from Mason, 1989; Ward, 1988)

Before drinking	Whilst drinking
1. Eat something beforehand.	1. Start off with a long soft drink.
2. Postpone going out.	2. Drink half units.
3. Don't drink in places where you have previously drunk heavily.	3. Dilute your alcoholic drinks.
4. Take little money.	4. Drink in sips (time yourself).
5. Take alcohol-free beverages with you.	5. Alternate between non-alcoholic and alcoholic beverages.
	6. Avoid standing at the bar.
	7. Do not eat crisps and peanuts as they will make you thirsty.
	8. Practise drinking refusal skills.
	9. Distract yourself whilst drinking (e.g. play darts, have a chat).
	10. Try to go home early.

Table 4.2 Controlled drinking programme (adapted from Velleman, 1992)

Key targets	What to remember	Strategic plan
1. Three days a week without a drink.	1. Alcohol-free days are Tuesday, Thursday and Sunday.	1. Eat something before you go out.
2. No drinking before 7 pm.	2. Problematic drinking is linked to wine, so all drinking will be limited to beer.	2. Do not take more than £10 with you.
3. No more than 3 units a day.		3. Practise drinking refusal strategies.
		4. Always start with a non-alcohol drink.
		5. Do something when you are there that does not involve only drinking.

practitioner and client should not forget alcohol's disinhibitory properties, which may cancel out the certainty of keeping to a prearranged limit once the first units have been drunk. Research suggests that people who are most successful at controlled drinking are those who are younger, are employed, have a family around them, have a short history of drinking problems, consume low levels before seeking help, and show no signs of physical dependence (Heather & Robertson, 1983; Ward, 1988).

ADDRESSING COMPLICATING PROBLEMS

Introduction

Problem drinking is often complicated by a variety of concomitant difficulties (as the assessment phases typically highlight) that interfere with the planning and outcomes of therapy. Some of these complicating problems will now be reviewed and recommendations for their management put forward.

Concomitant and co-morbid mental health problems

Research has indicated that a large proportion of those diagnosed with alcohol abuse or dependence (therefore a large proportion of problem drinkers) also experience other mental health problems, which may be concurrent with, antecedent to, or consequent to their drinking (Rosenthal & Westreich, 1999). In treatment settings at least 30–40% of clients are likely to report an alcohol use problem as part of their presenting problems (Helzer & Pryzbeck, 1988; Kushner et al., 1990; Wilson, 1988). The most common concomitant mental health problems are other psychoactive substance use disorders, anxiety disorders and mood disorders (Cooper et al., 1995; Miller et al., 2002). As a general rule clients with concomitant/co-morbid severe mental health problems (e.g. bipolar disorder and psychosis) should be treated in specialized treatment settings, whereas clients with mild to moderate mental health problems (e.g. anxiety disorders and major depressive disorder) can be treated in specialized alcohol (or general) treatment settings. Given the considerable heterogeneity in symptoms and course among individuals with concurrent/co-morbid mental health problems and problem drinking, it is recommended that planning of therapeutic interventions be based on a detailed case formulation. In most cases therapy should first target the drinking problem if this is severe, but for some clients the mental health problem may have priority, provided that alcohol use is well managed over time. In other clients simultaneous therapy for problem drinking and mental health problems may be recommended if both are relatively moderate in severity.

Anxiety disorders

Once it has been established whether an anxiety disorder is present, the practitioner should initially determine the temporal relationship between the anxiety disorder and problem drinking. In the case of some anxiety disorders (e.g. specific phobias) there is usually no need to ascertain temporal relationships since they typically run independent courses. With respect to other anxiety disorders (e.g. panic disorder and social anxiety disorder), it is crucial to establish whether these are related to problem drinking. For example, in the case of social anxiety disorder, alcohol is often used prior to entering social situations as a form of anxiolytic, and in the case of panic attacks these are often associated with withdrawal symptoms. The course of anxiety disorders and their relationship with problem drinking can usually be established retrospectively by using the Timeline Followback interview (Sobell et al., 1996).

It is also important to consider that frequently the association between an anxiety disorder and problem drinking is bidirectional. Since evidence suggests that problem drinking may perpetuate/exacerbate anxiety symptoms, it is advisable to observe changes in anxiety symptoms when alcohol use is discontinued or substantially reduced. Generally, CBT targeting problem drinking is also likely to result in a reduction in anxiety symptoms. If the anxiety symptoms are still present after a period of at least four weeks of abstinence or moderate drinking, there is a need to consider more detailed assessment and therapy directed toward the concomitant anxiety disorder.

CBT has a strong empirical basis supporting its efficacy in treating a range of anxiety disorders. Description of these interventions falls outside the scope of this book. For detailed clinical applications of the various approaches, the reader is referred to Hawton et al. (1989) and Wells (1997).

Mood disorders – dysthymia and major depression

The prevalence of depression is high in individuals with problem drinking and is usually associated with a complex clinical picture. When dealing with a client who presents with depression, it is important to bear in mind that depression could simply be an independent mental health problem with no functional relationship to problem drinking. In numerous cases, depressive symptoms are the consequence of prolonged drinking, whilst depressed mood can be the result of the withdrawal effects associated with chronic alcohol use. In both instances, depressive symptoms may retract after a reduction in alcohol use, and without requiring therapy targeting the depression. In a number of clients, however, depression may have preceded the onset of problem drinking or occurred during periods of abstinence, thus promoting use. In these cases one would expect a causal link between depression and problem drinking to be present. Typically clients may use alcohol to self-medicate depressive symptoms or be more vulnerable to stress during episodes of depression, losing control over alcohol use.

Given the complexity of the relationship between the causes and course of depression and problem drinking, each client requires a detailed assessment and case formulation to determine the sequence of depressed mood and problem drinking and to establish if indeed there is a causal link. Practitioners are advised to undertake prospective and retrospective monitoring to establish the nature of, and the fluctuations in, the symptoms of depression and problem drinking. As is the case with anxiety disorders, the Timeline Followback interview (Sobell et al., 1996) is particularly helpful in investigating potential causal relationships between depression and problem drinking.

In most cases where depression and problem drinking are concomitant, the same policy is recommended as discussed for managing concomitant anxiety disorders and problem drinking. If the level of depression allows (and the client does not display suicidal ideation and intentionality), it is advisable to observe changes in depressive symptoms when alcohol use is discontinued or substantially reduced. Generally, CBT targeting problem drinking is also likely to result in a reduction in depressive symptoms. If the symptoms of depression are still present after a period of at least four weeks of abstinence or moderate drinking, there is a need to consider more detailed assessment and therapy directed toward the concomitant mood disorder. CBT has strong empirical support for its efficacy in treating depression. Description of these interventions falls outside the scope of this book. For detailed clinical applications of the various approaches, the reader is referred to Beck (1995) and Hawton et al. (1989).

Mood disorders – bipolar disorder

Bipolar disorder and problem drinking occur more often than would be expected by chance. Bipolar disorder, often termed 'manic depression', is a mood disorder that is characterized by extreme fluctuations in mood (from euphoria to severe depression), interspersed with periods of euthymia (normal mood). There are a number of disorders in the bipolar spectrum, including: bipolar I disorder, bipolar II disorder and cyclothymia. Bipolar I disorder is the most severe and is characterized by manic episodes that last for at least a week and depressive episodes that last for at least two weeks. Clients who are fully manic often require hospitalization to decrease the risk of harming themselves or others. Individuals can also simultaneously suffer from depression and mania (this condition appears to be accompanied by a greater risk of suicide and is more difficult to treat). Bipolar II disorder is characterized by episodes of hypomania (a less severe form of mania) that last for at least four consecutive days and are not severe enough to require hospitalization. Hypomania is interspersed with depressive episodes that last at least 14 days. Cyclothymia is a disorder in the bipolar spectrum that is characterized by frequent low-level mood fluctuations that range from hypomania to low-level depression, with symptoms being present for at least two years (American Psychiatric Association, 1994).

There is little published data on specific pharmacologic and psychotherapeutic therapies for bipolar disorder in the presence of problem drinking. The general recommendation is to refer the client for sequential or concurrent therapy in a specialized treatment setting where the use of medications most frequently used in managing bipolar spectrum disorders (lithium and valproate) can be closely monitored, especially in consideration of evidence suggesting that clients presenting with concomitant drinking problems and bipolar spectrum disorders display different responses to medications (Prien, Himmelhoch, & Jupfer, 1988). Group intervention programmes have been developed (e.g. Weiss, Najavits, & Greenfield, 1999) specifically for clients with bipolar disorder and substance-use disorders. The goals of these programmes include education regarding the relationship between the substance use and bipolar disorder, provision of mutual support through group interactions, abstinence from substance use and adherence to prescribed medication regimens. Special emphasis is given to the advantages and disadvantages of taking medication for both bipolar disorder (e.g. mood stabilizers) and for substance-use disorders (e.g. naltrexone, disulfiram).

Suicide

Suicide and problem drinking are closely associated. Individuals who misuse alcohol are more likely to commit suicide than those who do not (Inskip, Harris, & Barraclough, 1998). The higher prevalence of suicide in problem drinkers is in part explained by the high prevalence of other mental health problems associated with suicide. In particular, antisocial personality disorder, borderline personality disorder and mood disorders. Other risk factors include: imprisonment, prolonged unemployment, sexual abuse and social isolation (Moscicki, 1997).

The assessment of current suicidal ideation and intentionality is an essential part of the assessment phase, especially so if concomitant disorders, such as depression and personality disorders, are identified. Further, it is important to investigate the history of violence and self-harm, as the latter is often associated with problem drinking and significantly increases the risk of suicide. Many suicides are also committed as an impulsive act when intoxicated, so it is important to closely monitor those with a recent history of suicide attempts, who have no close friends and who are using different drugs.

Personality disorders

Two personality disorders are common and may be overlooked in problem drinkers: antisocial personality disorder (APD) and borderline personality disorder (BPD). APD is characterized by a wide array of symptoms, including the failure to conform to social norms, disregarding safety of self and/or others, consistent irresponsibility, lack of remorse after having hurt, mistreated or stolen from others, irritability, recklessness and deceitfulness. Clients with APD frequently present with a fearful attachment style (Timmerman & Emmelkamp, 2006), which is characterized by avoidance of close relationships. This appears to be rooted in a fear of rejection, a sense of personal insecurity and a distrust of others. Many clients presenting with APD have a history of early traumatic experiences in which parental figures have often violated their trust in them. Furthermore, distrusting others may in some instances be of major importance in order to 'survive' (for example, in a criminal context).

Difficulties in the therapy of APD lie in the client's fear of trusting practitioners and of showing weaknesses. Brutal, manipulative and avoidant actions are often aimed at keeping others at an emotionally safe distance, implying, from a clinical perspective, that considerable effort and time are needed to build a strong therapeutic relationship. This relationship has to be fundamentally characterized by a safe environment in which the client can feel comfortable in being open about difficulties.

BPD is characterized by marked impulsivity, chronic feelings of emptiness, identity disturbance, difficulties in controlling anger, intense and frequent mood swings and life-threatening behaviours (e.g. self-injury and suicidal gestures). In problem drinkers, routine screening for BPD is clinically useful to identify clients with an increased risk of potentially fatal behaviours (e.g. binge drinking and suicide).

For severe forms of APD and BPD it is clinically wise to refer clients to specialist services. In the case of BPD, for example, dialectical behaviour therapy (DBT; Linehan, 1993) has shown to be effective. DBT comprises strategies from CBT and acceptance strategies adapted from mindfulness training. Over the last decade DBT has also been adapted for clients with drug dependence.

Psychotic disorders

The co-occurrence of problem drinking and psychotic disorders (especially schizophrenia) is recognized as a major problem within mental health care. Integrated therapy (Ziedonis et al., 2005) is recommended for schizophrenic clients with substance-use disorders, and requires integrating medications with CBT and motivational interviewing. Specific recommendations are provided concerning screening for substance-use disorders and selecting the most appropriate medications to maximize safety and minimize drug interactions, as well as assessing motivation for change, and managing medical conditions that commonly occur in such clients.

Intimate partner violence

The prevalence of intimate partner violence is higher among couples in which one or both partners are problem drinkers. Research suggests that behavioural couples therapy can result in a significant reduction in male-to-female physical aggression when compared with individual-based behavioural therapy (Fals-Stewart et al., 2005). This suggests that involving the assaulted partner in therapy may reduce the risk of violence.

When assessing clients, the topic of violence should never be omitted. On the whole, clients are reluctant to talk about this because of feelings of shame or fear of the negative consequences of disclosure. It is the task of the practitioner to ask detailed, non-judgemental questions about the violence and to gather as much data as is needed to make a balanced decision on whether to treat the client or refer them to an organization specialized in anger management. In dealing with intimate partner violence the following guidelines may be of help:

- if the violence only occurs under the influence of alcohol, is low in frequency and low to mild in severity, specific plans about how to prevent violence during a lapse/relapse can be made and therapy for problem drinking can commence. Violence should be addressed in every therapy session and assertiveness training and anger-management should be added to the therapy plan
- if the violence occurs with or without the influence of alcohol, specialized aggression-control therapy is needed. In addition, before starting, the practitioner must have a clear agreement with the client about which behaviours are tolerated and which are not

Homelessness

Therapeutic interventions discussed throughout this book are more suited for clients who live in safe environments with at least some supportive social contacts than for the homeless. In the case of homeless clients, the primary needs are food and shelter, and as long as these needs are not met, CBT for problem drinking is usually of very limited utility. At present, safe housing combined with community reinforcement in combination with contingency management is the recommended therapy programme for addressing this issue.

RELAPSE PREVENTION AND THE END OF THERAPY

Relapse prevention

Relapse can be broadly separated into the type that occurs quickly, during the early part of therapy, and the type that occurs later, following the termination of therapy. The first type of relapse usually arises because the client has tried to progress into the action phase (using the stages of change model as a framework) too quickly. That is before having given sufficient thought and time to issues of ambivalence. This section is concerned with the second type of relapse. This is relapse that occurs in the client who is high on motivation but cannot manage to put into practice their intentions. Why is this? According to Marlatt and Gordon (1985) it is because they may have not:

⊙ fully learned the skills that can help them effectively face situations that typically trigger alcohol use
⊙ explicitly and directly addressed the possibility of a lapse or relapse
⊙ reviewed what to do if a lapse occurs and prevent it from escalating into a fully-fledged relapse episode and
⊙ achieved a balanced lifestyle

These areas will now be reviewed.

Normalization and prevention of relapse

A central feature of the relapse prevention approach is discussing openly with the client the possibility of lapsing (a one-time return to drinking behaviour) and relapsing (a return to a lifestyle of problem drinking). Indeed many clients will already be aware of this and may well have gone through the stages of change several times. What is important to communicate to the client is that if a lapse does occur, it is not a catastrophe. One way of doing this is to review with the client the idea that the progress towards any human goal will never be linear, as we would sometimes expect it to be, and that if a lapse does occur it should be viewed as an integral part of what the client is working towards: continuing to practise abandoning old drinking behaviours and replacing these with new adaptive behaviours.

There are five steps (Marlatt & Gordon, 1985) which generally bring about a lapse (the first drink) and these should be reviewed with the client:

1 an apparently irrelevant decision that leads to
2 a high-risk situation in which the client has
3 a lack of appropriate skills to cope, which engenders
4 a sense of helplessness, diminished self-efficacy and low self-control, which in turn activates
5 positive expectancies that alcohol will help manage the situation

All the above areas have already been described in this book and should have been addressed in therapy. However, they will need to be reviewed, expanded and rehearsed as part of the goal of relapse prevention. One way of doing this is to ask the client to generate a personalized blueprint of the work done in therapy. The content of the blueprint should be guided by specific questions that will help the client review what they have learned and benefited from during therapy as well as highlight areas that need further consideration and analysis (particularly relapse prevention). These questions should follow sequentially through the history of the therapy experience:

1 What is problem drinking (its salient characteristics with respect to your own experience of it)?
2 What are the benefits and costs of drinking and the benefits and costs of not drinking?
3 What have you learned from the functional analysis about the mechanics of your problem and what are the salient features of your case formulation?
4 In which ways can you deal with stimulus conditions?
5 How can you effectively manage high-risk situations?
6 What skills will help you to manage your drinking behaviour, what was the effect of practising them, and which need to be further developed?

Table 4.3 Plan for managing high-risk situations

Situation	Response
Upcoming social event	(1) Assess risk ("Where?", "When?" "Who?); (2) decide on whether to go; (3) rehearse drinking refusal exchange; (4) maintain motivation by reviewing blueprint and continuing with pleasurable activities.
Old drinking pal	Avoid meeting where there's alcohol; and (2) only meet in safe circumstance (e.g. coffee at lunchtime).
Bored with work	(1) Remind myself that everyone gets bored with work sometimes; (2) do some motivating work (e.g. search database or "free" reading); (3) schedule pleasurable activity (e.g. running or cinema); and (4) review blueprint or use craving flashcard.
Criticism	(1) Remind myself that any anger or humiliation will go away over time; and (2) do an absorbing, pleasurable activity (e.g. film, novel, music, exercise).
Natural low	(1) Remind myself that it is normal to feel low from time to time and it will pass; (2) get out of bed; (3) exercise; (4) schedule pleasurable activities; and (5) review blueprint or use craving flashcard.

7 In which ways can you manage unhelpful beliefs and negative emotion?
8 In which ways can partners, family members and friends help with problem drinking?
9 What complicating factors need addressing and reviewing?

Table 4.3 is a sample plan for dealing with warning signals of a possible lapse/relapse. This was developed by reviewing a personalized blueprint and identifying areas that needed to be further strengthened.

Management of relapse

According to Marlatt and Gordon (1985), breaking abstinence is likely to lead to a full relapse because of the abstinence violation effect mentioned in Chapter 1. Clients must therefore be persuaded not to view a slip as a personal failure, but (as highlighted earlier) as a learning experience and something that can be avoided in the future. The following strategies (adapted from Marlatt & Gordon, 1985) can be used by clients to cope with a lapse:

⊙ stop drinking and delay further drinking – if a slip occurs the client should stop (for 1 to 2 hours) drinking and observe what is happening. The slip is a consequence of not having properly acknowledged a high-risk situation

- removing yourself from the situation – the client should as soon as is practically possible leave the situation where the slip occurred
- avoiding panicking – the client's instinctive reaction to a slip may be to blame themselves and feel extremely guilty about what's happened. This reaction is normal and the client needs to have cues (for example, a flashcard) that will remind them that every negative emotion will eventually subside, including this one
- recalling what has been achieved to date – the client should return to their blueprint and think back over the reasons that made them decide to change their drinking behaviour
- analysing the situation that brought about the slip – the client should attempt to immediately focus on what brought about the slip and warning signals that preceded it
- kick-starting the recovery – the client should get back in action by reviewing all the strategies for avoiding relapse
- seeking help – the client should ask their friends, family or partner to help in any way they can. If alone, the client should seek out the assistance of professionals or self-help groups

Achieving a balanced lifestyle

It has been suggested that long-term success in managing problem drinking is dependent on positive lifestyle changes that allow for a balance between responsibilities and pleasure to be achieved (Marlatt & Gordon, 1985). As the client begins to change, they may wish to make up for time lost in their lives or lack of responsibility by taking on high levels of responsibility with family, home and work. The first thing the practitioner should do is help the client identify areas in their life that may need to be more balanced. These may include: interpersonal relationships, employment and finances, physical health, exercise and nutrition. The client can be asked to think ahead over the next few months and list the difficulties they may have to deal with in these areas. These could be related to starting a new job, a house move, sorting out their finances or the birth of a baby. Once this is done the client should write down ways in which these difficulties might be tackled. It is crucial to ensure that the client draws on what they have learned from therapy.

Whatever the client decides to do with respect to achieving a more balanced lifestyle, they should be reminded to do it in a gradual manner to avoid raising expectations excessively. As clients begin to change and feel better, they may have surges of energy characterized by the need to make up for 'lost time'. This may result in them taking on numerous responsibilities in one go: getting a new job, moving into a new home, re-training, engaging in major redecoration, cleaning out 20 years' worth of mess and so on. This enthusiasm for responsibility can be a double-edged sword: satisfying but also very tiring and unrewarding. At times, too much responsibility may end up leading the client to question the value of not drinking. It is of paramount importance not to forget to help the client continue to schedule pleasurable activities in their life.

End of therapy

Ideally therapy will end when the client has successfully achieved their goals. In practice, ending is often not so straightforward because the process of goal-setting, exploration and action is continuous. Hence therapy ends not when all goals have been achieved but when the client has mastered the processes they must go through in order to find adaptive solutions to their problems; when they are capable of regulating their own behaviour. A further reason why the end of therapy can be complicated is the therapeutic relationship itself. It is not unusual for a client to become dependent on the practitioner and it can happen that new problems arise, or relapse occurs as a means of retaining the therapeutic relationship. The converse is true, as practitioners can become attached to a client and may find it difficult to give them up. It is in clinical supervision where many of these issues will need to be reviewed. The end of therapy is the time for the client and practitioner to review progress made. This is done by:

⊙ reviewing what was covered during therapy
⊙ providing feedback to the client on his/her progress
⊙ getting the client's feedback on the most useful aspects of therapy
⊙ setting longer-term objectives and
⊙ planning for emergencies

Areas covered

The practitioner should review with the client the three areas covered during therapy (preparation, implementation and maintenance of change) with a view to facilitating the development of a personalized blueprint of the experience of therapy. The content of the blueprint should be guided by specific questions that will help the client review what they have learned and benefited from during therapy (see page 124 Normalization and prevention of relapse).

Practitioner's feedback

The practitioner should feed back to the client the progress made with a strong emphasis on the positive as well as highlighting areas that warrant further intervention. It is advisable to use a very empathic style on the lines of the motivational interventions highlighted earlier.

Client's feedback

It is equally important for the practitioner to elicit feedback from the client on progress made during therapy and what was found to be most helpful. It is also important for the practitioner to discover the client's concerns about the ending of therapy. Again, the use of a highly empathic style is recommended.

Longer-term objectives

The practitioner and client should discuss what the client would want their life to look like in the future and what steps may need to be taken for this to happen. This discussion should include the delineation of the steps to be taken, how they would be measured, whether they are realistic and within what timeframe they can be achieved. The client should also be encouraged to focus on one area of change at a time unless a radical lifestyle change is justified.

Planning for emergencies

Apart from reviewing all the work done on relapse prevention and having a system in place to deal with future high-risk situations, the practitioner and client need to decide what will be done if a fully-fledged relapse occurs. Key areas to cover include available support from significant others or the community, and access to an emergency phone number and hospital in the event of a severe drinking episode. As described earlier, clients who present with problem drinking may also present with a myriad of complicating problems. At the end of therapy, the practitioner should consider and review the impact of possible problems related to housing, transport, employment, the legal system, the family, childcare, medical conditions and concurrent mental health problems. Knowledge of agencies and services in the local community is essential for an effective interfacing with other health and social systems. Finally, the role of self-help groups should be considered as an option for maintaining and improving gains made in therapy.

CHAPTER 5

Practitioner training and clinical supervision

TRAINING

A CBT practitioner needs to be properly trained. Typically, training requirements for developing CBT competencies are determined by national professional organizations, which outline standards that need to be met in order to become an accredited practitioner in the delivery of psychosocial therapies. Delivering the CBT interventions described in this book will require a minimum level of competency in CBT. Furthermore, training in CBT ideally needs to be supplemented by experience in core counselling and motivational skills, and in working with problem drinkers.

CLINCIAL SUPERVISION

Clinical supervision is central to the practice of CBT. The functions of clinical supervision are several, as Lewis (2005) suggests:

- to encourage and support the practitioner
- to act as an early warning system for poor and unsafe practice
- to engender awareness and reflective practice
- to encourage and facilitate the practitioner's continuing professional development and education

In line with Kolb's learning cycle (1984), clinical supervision should ideally be an experiential learning activity in which a concrete experience is the focus of observation and analysis, resulting in a conceptualization of the experience in terms of abstract ideas and generalizations. This, in turn, leads to testing the implications of these ideas and generalizations in new contexts, which in itself become a concrete experience to be reflected upon. Continuing with Kolb's learning cycle as a framework, the areas that would be the focus of observation and analysis in clinical supervision would include:

- the client's presenting problems and goals
- the functional analyses, case formulation and therapeutic interventions

⊙ ethical and professional issues, including power imbalances, prejudices and differences in culture and/or ethnicity
⊙ the impact of the client and/or nature of therapy on the practitioner's wellbeing
⊙ the context of therapeutic activity (e.g. demands of organizations)
⊙ the therapeutic relationship

Feedback on the practitioner's implementation of CBT

Receiving feedback on the implementation of CBT is fundamental to the practitioner because:

⊙ it fosters greater adherence to the CBT protocols (through an increased emphasis on self-monitoring)
⊙ it acts as a reminder of the key active ingredients of CBT and
⊙ it generates a useful record of which therapeutic interventions were administered and how well this was done

Having a relatively objective basis on which to evaluate the practitioner's implementation of CBT is fundamental. Together with direct or indirect (e.g. audiovisual material) observations of a therapy session and the traditional reporting of cases, evaluation of therapy sessions can be achieved through the clinical supervisor and the practitioner completing therapy rating scales. Examples of this include the CBT Therapist Checklist (Carroll, 1998), which was originally developed for cocaine dependence therapy but can easily be adapted to problem drinking, and the Cognitive Therapy Scale Revised (CTS-R; Blackburn et al., 2001), which focuses on general CBT skills.

Rating scales provide structured feedback to the practitioner and form the basis of clinical supervision. They also provide a method of determining whether a practitioner in training is ready to be accredited in delivering CBT.

Frequency of clinical supervision

The level and intensity of clinical supervision will reflect the availability of resources and the experience and skill of the practitioner. For an experienced practitioner, the minimum acceptable level of ongoing clinical supervision should be one hour once a month, though this could be more in cases where workloads are very heavy. For a less experienced practitioner, one hour once a week is recommended. These recommendations are based on the assumption clinical supervision is delivered on a one-to-one basis. If this is not the case, a further 45 minutes will be needed for each additional practitioner. Clinical supervision will be more effective if conducted in a consistent place and at a regular time. Goals will need to be clarified, roles defined, and evaluation procedures outlined and agreed.

Common problems encountered in clinical supervision

The structure of CBT sessions is aimed at integrating therapeutic interventions with a supportive practice that meets the specific needs of each client. Less experienced practitioners, in particular those with limited exposure to working with problem drinking and unaccustomed to high levels of structure in therapy, frequently allow therapy sessions to become unfocused. By and large such practitioners delay the introduction of therapeutic interventions until the latter part of the therapy session. This results in rushing through important material and often failing to use client examples or get feedback. Other practitioners, who may be competent in CBT but have limited experience of working with problem drinkers, may allow themselves to become overwhelmed by alcohol-related crises presented by the client. This typically leads to failing to focus on essential therapeutic interventions aimed at helping the client to learn to avoid or manage crises. In the longer term, a crises-driven approach will undermine self-efficacy and fuel negative emotion. Conversely, maintaining a reasonably balanced and consistent structure in the therapy session will help to model effective coping skills.

On the other side of the spectrum, it is possible for a practitioner to become overly rigid in their application of CBT principles and protocols. This is typically fuelled by the ambition to get things absolutely right. It is important to remind such practitioners that a manual or guide is not set in stone and should be viewed with a degree of flexibility. This, however, often requires substantial familiarity with the material at both a theoretical and practical level, so that the practitioner can tailor it to the needs of the client in a manner that is fresh and dynamic.

Failing to get feedback from the client, to ensure that they have understood the material, is an additional and very common error made by many practitioners. As a rule, for each concept presented, the practitioner should stop to ask the client to provide, in their own words, an example or description of the idea. The practitioner should also attempt to explain CBT principles using specific examples. However, some practitioners are not clear, or assure themselves that clients have understood the concepts put forward. A typical example of this is problem-solving on the client's behalf rather than running systematically through the problem-solving procedure with them. Furthermore, just as some practitioners do not communicate clearly underlying principles, others fail to make the best use of the material presented by the client to illustrate their points.

Finally, though most clients undertake their out-of-therapy session assignments, many practitioners do not attend to these in enough detail, for example, by only superficially reviewing assignments at the beginning of a therapy session or rushing through them at the end. Practitioners and clients are by no means limited to the out-of-therapy session assignments suggested in this guide. Indeed, it is preferable for a client to generate their own exercises.

CASE EXAMPLE

In this section a synopsis of a case is presented to illustrate the application of CBT for problem drinking.

Biographic details

John (pseudonym) is a single 35-year-old man. He was born in Chelmsford, United Kingdom. At present he works in the advertising industry, in the same company he joined when he was 28 years old. Both his father and mother are alive and he keeps in contact with them regularly, describing their relationship as good. He has an older brother who lives in Australia but to whom he still talks regularly. His General Practitioner referred him for alcohol abuse and mood problems.

Assessment

Assessment, which took place over a two-hour session, began with collecting basic background information. John had no medical conditions of note and was not using medication. He had never been diagnosed with a mental health problem nor had ever been prescribed medication. In 2000 he saw a counsellor (self-referred) for eight sessions. He found the experience useful but felt it did not provide him with enough skills to tackle his problems. His main goal in therapy was to reduce his alcohol use.

John then completed a batch of self-report measures to determine the presence, severity and impact of the drinking problem. He first completed the Alcohol Use Disorders Identification Test (AUDIT; Babor et al., 1992) on which he scored 12, indicating the presence of an alcohol use problem unlikely to be severe enough to qualify as alcohol dependence. This was corroborated by:

- the fact that he did not report daily/regular and morning drinking and
- a score of 10 on the Alcohol Dependence Scale (ADS; Skinner & Allen, 1982).

Quantity and frequency of alcohol use was determined using the Timeline Followback interview (Sobell et al., 1996). This revealed John had drunk alcohol on average 3–4 days a week over the previous 6 months. His preferred beverages were beer and vodka, and he reported that the most he drank on any one day was 12 units. His consumption was in the range of 6–12 units on a typical drinking day. John had been drinking since 2003 in a manner defined by him as 'concerning'. He also stated that his drinking had become progressively worse in frequency (originally once or twice a week, and at present three or four times a week) and impact (from 2–3 drinks per occasion to up to 12 now).

To attain an overview of his mental health state, John was then administered the Beck Anxiety Inventory (BAI; Beck et al., 1988) on which he scored 8, and the Beck Depression Inventory (BDI; Beck et al., 1961) on which he scored 20, respectively, indicating low to mild levels of anxiety and the presence of significant depressive symptomatology.

Responses on the Life Stressors and Social Resources Inventory (LISRES; Moos et al., 1988) indicated two key problem areas: friends and social activities, and work. These areas would be explored in more detail in the case formulation phase.

Finally John's motivation for change was assessed by administering the Stages of Change and Therapy Eagerness Scale (SOCRATES; Miller & Tonigan, 1996). This indicated that John recognized he had a problem with alcohol use and was taking steps to modify and address it, but was still feeling ambivalent about changing his behaviour.

Enhancing motivation for change

As John reported ambivalence about drinking, motivational exercises were introduced over the course of the following two sessions. These helped John make a greater commitment to modifying his drinking behaviour as well as consider in detail concerns regarding change (for example, not knowing how to cope with low mood).

Case formulation

Presenting problems as stated by the client

The case formulation process began by asking John to summarize, in his own words, the difficulties he was experiencing. He was encouraged to explain how he saw his problems, not how others (e.g. family, friends and professionals) perceived them. Specific problem statements were sought because they form the foundation upon which goals of therapy are operationalized. John stated that his main problems were:

Problem 1: Increasingly out-of-control drinking
John reported (reiterating what emerged from the assessment phase) that he drank heavily 3–4 times a week when at home alone. Over the course of the last decade the drinking had "slowly got worse". Recently he passed out, following what he described as a "long binge" lasting from Sunday afternoon until evening. He also stated that his drinking was becoming increasingly difficult to control, but he still felt he could refrain from drinking for a week or more if he needed to. He felt an urge to drink when he was feeling "low" and when "thoughts were running in his head".

Problem 2: Low mood
John reported frequently "feeling down" and "tired". He said that at best he was feeling low 60% of the time with peaks of 70–80% during the winter months. He reported that he felt "empty" and increasingly spent time "brooding" about his life and "putting off doing things", especially at work. He had frequent thoughts such as "What's the point of it all?", "I've never achieved anything", "I feel alone". John also reported that his interest in work and recreational activities had been declining over the last 2–3 years.

Therapy goals as stated by the client

At this point John was encouraged to outline what changes he hoped for. These were:

Goal 1: Gain greater control of drinking
John stated he would like to reduce substantially his alcohol consumption to a "social and controlled drinking" level. He thought that 20 units a week would be a realistic target compared with the 40–50 units that he had been consuming. This goal had been in his mind for some time, but was 'cemented' through the motivational exercises.

Goal 2: Improve mood
John explained that he would like to feel most of the time in a "decent" mood; that is, limiting feeling low to 10–20% of the time, at least to begin with. He appreciated that episodes of low mood were integral to life, but stated he would want to learn how to "manage them better". This, he believed, would also make him feel better about his job and help him re-engage with it.

Functional analysis of the presenting problems

At this juncture, functional analyses of the presenting problems were undertaken. The first functional analysis was of drinking behaviour (see Table 5.1). This identified that John was drinking primarily to regulate negative thoughts and associated low mood occurring when alone at home. Drinking was reinforced by providing "numbing" of the negative thoughts, and the alleviation of craving and low mood (maintaining consequences). The problem consequences identified related to the escalation of thoughts about the uncontrollability of alcohol use, lowering of self-esteem and a worsening of mood brought about by alcohol's depressogenic properties.

Based on John's account of his difficulties, it appeared that low mood was exacerbated by alcohol use but triggered by:

⊙ negative thoughts about loneliness and
⊙ negative thoughts about work challenges (in line with what emerged from the assessment phase)

For reasons of clarity, two distinct functional analyses of low mood were presented: the first (Table 5.2), low mood linked to thoughts about loneliness; the second (Table 5.3), low mood linked to thoughts about work challenges. The functional analysis of low mood linked to thoughts about loneliness indicated that John was engaging in a maladaptive coping strategy (brooding) to regulate these negative thoughts and associated low mood that primarily occurred when he was alone at home. Brooding was reinforced by providing a distraction from negative thoughts and associated alleviation of low mood (maintaining consequences). The problem consequences identified related to the escalation of thoughts about the perseveration of low mood, a reduction in engagement (exercise, socializing) and a precipitation of mood.

The functional analysis of low mood linked to thoughts about work challenges indicated that John was engaging in maladaptive coping strategies (procrastination and engagement in menial tasks) to regulate negative thoughts (and associated low mood) occurring at work when facing challenging tasks. These coping strategies were reinforced by providing a distraction from the negative thoughts and associated alleviation of low mood (maintaining consequences). The problem consequences identified related to the escalation of thoughts about the perseveration of procrastination and associated lowering of mood, a reduction in self-esteem and self-efficacy, and growing criticisms from colleagues for not getting his work done. At this stage, the circularity of John's problems started to become apparent. From the two functional analyses relating to low mood, it was evident that the coping strategies employed both at work and at home alone contributed to a worsening of mood, which was primarily managed through using alcohol. However, using alcohol further sensitized John to experiencing negative thoughts and associated lows in mood, locking him into a vicious cycle.

Integrated developmental profiling

This stage was aimed at understanding the circumstances and conditions in which the problems started and their 'evolution' to present date.

John stated that he had always had ups and downs in mood, but they began getting noticeably worse in his mid twenties (10 years ago) following the ending of a 5-year romantic relationship that had begun at university. He recalled gradually giving up exercise, which had been a prominent part of his life until then, and spending increasing amounts of time reviewing what had gone wrong in this relationship. Though he made friends and had several romantic relationships, they failed to achieve any significant longevity. John recalled that around 5 years ago (aged 30) he started drinking more heavily (6–8 units a session) once or twice a week. The drinking then started escalating gradually to current levels. There were periods when he managed to drink little or nothing at all, and other periods when the frequency of drinking reached 5 days a week. Over the course of the last year, John began to lose interest in work

Table 5.1 Functional analysis of out-of-control drinking (FA1)

	Stimuli	Organism	Responses	Maintaining consequences	Problem consequences
Environmental	Alone at home				
Cognitive	"I feel low"; "Another day wasted"; "I am a loser"	"Let's have one"; "It will turn my mind off"		"Numbing" of negative thoughts	Thoughts about the uncontrollability of alcohol use and lowering of self-esteem
Physiological		Craving		Alleviation of craving	
Behavioural		Instrumental behaviours aimed at attaining alcohol	Drinking		
Emotional	Very low mood			Alleviation of low mood	Worsening of mood

Table 5.2 Functional analysis of low mood linked to thoughts about loneliness (FA2)

	Stimuli	Organism	Responses	Maintaining consequences	Problem consequences
Environmental	Alone at home				
Cognitive	"I feel alone"; "I feel low"; "I have not achieved anything"	"I ought to figure out why"; "Brooding will help"	Brooding	Distraction from negative thoughts	Thoughts about the perseveration of low mood
Physiological					
Behavioural					Reduction in engagement
Emotional	Low mood			Alleviation of low mood	Precipitation of mood

Table 5.3 Functional analysis of low mood linked to thoughts about work challenges (FA3)

	Stimuli	Organism	Responses	Maintaining consequences	Problem consequences
Environmental	Challenging tasks at work				Criticisms from colleagues for work not being accomplished
Cognitive	"It is difficult"; "There is so much to do"; "How will I manage"	"I will do things later"; "I will wait to be in a good mood to do things"	Procrastination	Distraction from negative thoughts	Thoughts about the uncontrollability of procrastination and lowering of self-esteem and efficacy
Physiological					
Behavioural			Engagement in menial tasks		
Emotional	Low mood			Alleviation of low mood	Lowering of mood

and to put things off for as long as he could. He attributed this to a general loss of interest in life.

Problem formulation

Information from the preceding sections was brought together in the problem formulation. This was shared with John and modified accordingly.

Before his mid 20s, John appeared to be functioning adaptively. He graduated from university with a first-class degree and did a masters course before commencing his career in the advertising industry. He did not drink excessively nor did he remember displaying any depressive symptomatology. Following the ending of a long-term romantic relationship, John began withdrawing: stopping exercise and socially distancing himself. In addition, he started spending increasing amounts of time alone at home brooding about his past, which fed back into his declining mood and worsened it. Over time, the combination of a reduction of rewarding activities and the engagement in an unhelpful coping strategy (brooding) led to a downward spiral in mood. To cope with this, John started using alcohol, which provided negative reinforcement through a temporary improvement in mood, distraction from negative thoughts and the interruption of brooding. John learned that, at least as a short-term coping strategy, his mental state could be controlled by drinking. As a longer term consequence of heavy alcohol use, however, his mood started worsening and he began experiencing bouts of self-doubt. As a consequence of this, when facing challenging tasks at work he would procrastinate and engage in menial tasks. Though reinforcing in the short-term, these coping strategies served to lower his mood further, contributing to the development of problem drinking.

The above problem formulation was presented to John together with the links between the different functional analyses presented (see Figure 5.1). It was also explained to him that the problem formulation was a working hypothesis that needed to be tested out in order to prove its validity. John broadly agreed with it.

Collaborative definition of therapy goals

Following the presentation and discussion of the problem formulation, the therapy goals were agreed with John. These were modified (in terms of

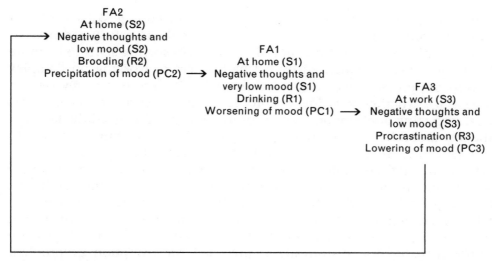

FA2
At home (S2)
Negative thoughts and
low mood (S2)
Brooding (R2)
Precipitation of mood (PC2) →

FA1
At home (S1)
Negative thoughts and
very low mood (S1)
Drinking (R1)
Worsening of mood (PC1) →

FA3
At work (S3)
Negative thoughts and
low mood (S3)
Procrastination (R3)
Lowering of mood (PC3)

N.B. 'S' stands for the stimulus; 'R' stands for response; 'PC' stands for problem consequence.

Figure 5.1 Interlinking of the functional analyses in a problem formulation

order of importance and specificity) in view of the information that was gathered through the functional analyses and integrated in the case formulation. They are presented below:

Goal 1: Improvement in mood
To engage at work through achieving a balance between menial tasks on the one hand, and challenging and rewarding tasks on the other.
To learn how to interrupt brooding.
To increase fitness levels.
To build a portfolio of engaging recreational activities.

Goal 2: Reduction in drinking
To reduce alcohol consumed to a maximum of 30 units a week.
To consider abstaining from drinking for a period of time.

Development of the therapeutic programme

In this phase, and consistent with the problem formulation and collaborative definition of therapy goals, the rationale for the therapeutic programme was presented to John.

From the information gathered, it appeared that John had managed to drink moderately or be abstinent for long stretches of his life (until he was aged 30, he drank moderately). Deficiencies in coping skills were not evident. John did not report having had problems refusing drinks or asserting his needs. He also believed his problem-solving skills to be more than adequate, as evidenced by his past successes working on complex advertising projects that required these skills. We decided to review at a later stage whether focusing on problem-solving within other contexts (e.g. managing one's mood) may be of use. We also discussed the fact that the low mood he was experiencing may have been affecting his ability to problem-solve, so an improvement in mood may naturally result in a 're-activation' of these skills. Strategies for tackling the drinking problem would thus primarily focus on learning to identify stimulus conditions (which John had already began doing through the functional analyses), tackling craving, modifying beliefs and most importantly of all managing low mood. It was hypothesized that the latter area was of primary importance because historically it preceded the inception of problem drinking. The main thrust of therapy, outside of therapeutic interventions aimed at implementing change in drinking behaviour, would be on behavioural activation and the interruption of maladaptive coping strategies (brooding and procrastination).

Stage 1: Therapeutic interventions for low mood
It was agreed that, to begin with, behavioural strategies would be employed to improve mood (Hawton et al., 1989). These would focus primarily on monitoring activities through the use of a diary and engaging in graded mood-enhancing tasks (exercise, for example). With respect to procrastination, it was also agreed that tasks that were being postponed should be ranked in terms of difficulty and a commitment to engage in them in a graded way be made. Cognitive strategies (Beck, 1995), such as verbal reattribution and the Socratic Method, would be employed to challenge negative thoughts (triggers for brooding, procrastination and drinking). In addition to these content-focused strategies, a variety of metacognitive-focused interventions (Wells, 2000) would be employed to tackle brooding and procrastination, including: verbal reattribution of positive beliefs about rumination (Papegorgiou & Wells, 2003) and procrastination (Fernie & Spada, 2008), and attention training (Papageorgiou & Wells, 2000).

Stage 2: Therapeutic interventions for problem drinking
This phase of therapy would focus on self-monitoring drinking behaviour through the use of a diary. In the first therapy sessions the negative physical and psychological effects of problem drinking would be

illustrated and reviewed. Subsequently, interventions for identifying and managing stimulus conditions, tackling craving and modifying beliefs would be introduced in this order. It would be anticipated that the benefits of the strategies aimed at improving mood and interrupting brooding and procrastination would filter through and affect functioning to such an extent that John would realize that further improvements in mood could be attained if he were to reduce or stop drinking.

Monitoring change

A variety of measures were employed, at regular intervals, to monitor change. These included measures employed during assessment, activity and drinking diaries, and specific measures to assess metacognitions linked to rumination (Papageorgiou & Wells, 2001) and procrastination (Fernie et al., 2009).

Course of therapy

During the first five therapy sessions, John progressed swiftly through the various stages of assessment, motivational enhancement, case formulation and delineation of the therapeutic intervention programme. John appeared motivated and engaged. He displayed a natural understanding and affinity with the CBT rationale. During the course of this period, John's drinking patterns remained unchanged with his mood showing some, albeit small, improvement. This was expected to a certain extent because of the exploratory phase of therapy.

During the following five therapy sessions, John was encouraged to monitor his activities and drinking behaviour, and engage gradually in mood-elevating tasks. John filled his activity and drinking diaries consistently and agreed to write a list of 'things to do with his time outside work'. In this list he emphasized the desire to reintroduce physical activity into his life and to find things to do after work that would be socially engaging (e.g. attending dancing lessons, attending a language course). Amongst his weekly tasks we also decided to break down demanding activities at work into smaller units, and rank them in terms of difficulty with a view to begin to engage with them in a graded manner. By the end of the month, John had begun engaging in activities outside work regularly twice a week. He was also managing to get many more things done at work. In the therapy sessions, much of the focus was on cognitive and metacognitive interventions for low mood, brooding and procrastination, together with reviewing in greater detail stimulus conditions that led to drinking. It was identified that on certain days of the week (Wednesday, Thursday and Friday) and at certain times (between 6 pm and 8 pm), drinking was typically initiated. It was therefore decided that it would be best to schedule physical activity and social engagements during these days. John also developed a craving card and out-of-session assignments on restructuring beliefs related to alcohol use.

Between the 11th and 14th sessions, John started regularly reporting the positive impact on his mood of the various therapeutic interventions His mood had lifted considerably and he reported he had not felt low for 60% of the time. During this phase, John continued to drink but at a reduced level of around 25 units a week.

Around the 16th week, John stopped using alcohol. He decided to target abstinence, as he thought it would further improve his mood. During this period he managed to achieve most of the tasks set and discussed how he saw his problem mainly rooted in his mood, and actions he could take to modify it. John remained abstinent for two weeks, before experiencing two small 'slips'. However, these slips did not occur in the original context (at home alone) but in the company of people. On both occasions, John drank around 6 units.

For the remainder of therapy (a further four sessions), John was abstinent. He reported he had not felt as good for a long time and that he was concerned about 'coping' with potential 'lows' or 'obstacles' as well as his own irrational, maladaptive and obsolete thoughts. Over the last two sessions a relapse prevention plan for both low mood and drinking was put in place.

Outcome of therapy

At the end of therapy, scores on all self-report measures indicated marked improvements in functioning. AUDIT (Babor et al., 1992) stood at 3 (compared with 12 at the beginning of therapy), indicating no presence of problem drinking. Examination of the quantity and frequency of alcohol use revealed that John had drunk alcohol on average 1 day a week over the previous 2 months (compared with 3–4 days in the 6 months before therapy began). The maximum he had consumed in a single session was 6 units (compared with 12 prior to therapy). His consumption was in the range of 0–6 units on a typical drinking day compared with 6–12 before therapy. The Beck Anxiety Inventory (BAI; Beck et al., 1988), on which he scored 8 originally, was almost unchanged at 6. On the Beck Depression Inventory (BDI; Beck et al., 1961) on which he originally scored 20, he now scored 9, indicating no significant presence of depressive symptomatology. Responses on the Life Stressors and Social Resources Inventory (LISRES; Moos et al., 1988) indicated that the two original problem areas (friends and social activities, and work) had retracted to a non-problem status. Finally, John's motivation for change was re-assessed by administering the Stages of Change and Therapy Eagerness Scale (SOCRATES; Miller & Tonigan, 1996), which indicated that he recognized he had a problem with alcohol use and was taking steps to modify and address it, with ambivalence about changing his behaviour having reduced considerably from pre-therapy levels.

Activity diaries at the beginning of therapy showed that though pleasure ratings were on average moderate (roughly 5/10), 30% were under the 4 threshold. In addition, John spent most of his evenings at home (80%). At the end of therapy, John's pleasure ratings rose to an average of 7/10, with all but one score at or above 5. Time spent at home in the evenings had declined to 30%.

Appendices: Blank diaries and worksheets with instructions

Appendix A *Drinking diary*

Drinking Diary						
Week:	Morning	Units	Afternoon	Units	Evening	Units	Total units
Monday							
Tuesday							
Wednesday							
Thursday							
Friday							
Saturday							
Sunday							

Appendix B *Drinking decisional balance sheet*

Drinking Decisional Balance Sheet			
Continuing to drink		Making a change to my drinking	
Benefits	Costs	Benefits	Costs

Appendix C *Problems and goals*

Problems and Goals	
Problems	Goals

Step 1
In the left-hand column under the heading 'Problems', the client should draw up a detailed list of all the difficulties they encounter because of problem drinking.

Step 2
Transforming problems into goals is a crucial and helpful first step in overcoming any drinking problem. The client needs to appreciate that just thinking about their problem will not offer a solution or direction for getting better. The client therefore needs to set goals that will give them something concrete to aim for.

In the right-hand column of the worksheet under the heading 'Goals', the client should list one or more goals for each problem that they have identified. These will signal, once they are reached, that they are progressing towards overcoming the problem. Goals need to be made as specific as possible because if they are too general the client will not recognize they have reached them.

Appendix D   *Advantages of changing, concerns of changing and responses to concerns*

Advantages of Changing, Concerns of Changing and Responses to Concerns		
Advantages	Concerns	Responses to concerns
Outcome		

Step 1

In the first column of the worksheet, under the heading 'Advantages', the client should list all the advantages of changing that come to mind. The practitioner should ensure they take into account all the problems that have been identified in the 'Problems and Goals' exercise. As change will have an impact on many areas of life, the client needs to think how it might positively affect, in both the short term and long term, friendships, health, career, relationships and family.

Step 2

Once advantages have been identified, the client should move on to the second column, 'Concerns'. In this column, they should list all their concerns about change. The practitioner needs to ensure that the client considers all the problems that have been highlighted in the 'Problems and Goals' exercise. Could change have a negative impact on friendships, health, career, relationships and family? Both immediate concerns and longer-term negative outcomes of change should be considered.

Step 3

Once the list has been completed, the client should take some time to consider carefully what this exercise suggests. It may be that the advantages of change greatly outweigh any concerns the client may have. Conclusions should be noted at the bottom of the worksheet under the heading 'Outcome'.

Step 4

The client will have identified at least one concern, if not several, about change. It is usually helpful to examine these in greater detail so that they do not get in the way of commitment to change. Using the third column on the worksheet, the client should respond to concerns. When doing this, the following questions will aid the process:

"What would be another way of looking at this?"
"Is there any evidence that this may happen?"
"Do possible long-term advantages outweigh this risk, worry or problem?"
"If this is likely to be a real problem, how will you deal with it?"

Step 5

Once the client has responded to any concerns, they should re-run through the initial conclusions written at the bottom of the worksheet under the heading 'Outcome'. Is there anything more to add?

Appendix E *Examining specific change concerns*

Examining Specific Change Concerns	
What do you predict will happen?	
How likely is it to happen? (0–100%)	
Evidence for	Evidence against
Outcome	
How likely do you think it is now that this will happen? (0–100%)	
Conclusions	

Step 1
At the top of the worksheet the client should write down a concern they have about changing and what they predict will happen if they overcome their drinking problem. The client should be as specific as possible and ensure that they write down what they think is the very worst thing that may occur.

Step2
In the section underneath, the client should rate how likely they think it is that the worst will actually happen using a scale from 0 to 100% (0 being 'not at all likely' and 100 being 'extremely likely').

Step 3
Under the heading 'Evidence for', the client should list all the evidence they have that their concern is realistic.

Step 4
Under the heading 'Evidence against', the client should record all the evidence that suggests that their concern may not be realistic. The following questions may be useful when assessing the evidence for specific concerns:

"Have there been times when you thought this and it turned out not to be the case?"
"What would your best friend say about this?"
"Are you just focusing on the negatives because you are feeling down?"

Step 5
Once the task is completed, the client should reflect on how realistic their concern appears to be now. To get a more concrete idea, the concern should be re-rated on the 0 to 100% scale.

Appendix F *Functional analysis*

	Stimuli	Organism	Responses	Maintaining consequences	Problem consequences
Environmental					
Cognitive					
Physiological					
Behavioural					
Emotional					

Appendix G *Activating event breakdown*

Activating Event Breakdown						
Date	Time	Drink	Amount	Situation	Thoughts	Emotion

Appendix H *Evidence for and against the uncontrollability of craving*

Evidence For and Against the Uncontrollability of Craving	
Craving belief	Strength of belief (0–100%)
Evidence for	Evidence against
Outcome	
Re-rating of belief in each thought (0–100%)	

Step 1
At the top of the worksheet the client should write down typical uncontrollability beliefs they hold about craving.

Step 2
The strength of belief should be rated on a scale from 0 to 100%.

Step 3
The client should then ask themselves what evidence there is for and against the belief. Typical evidence may include:

⦿ drinking every time craving is experienced
⦿ not being able to do anything else when experiencing craving and
⦿ behaving in a crazed way when experiencing craving

The client needs to ensure that they make a list of all this evidence under the heading 'Evidence for'. The next step is to examine this evidence more carefully. The practitioner should highlight the possibility that the client may be misinterpreting evidence relevant to their craving. The questions to ask the client in order to challenge the evidence for lack of control over craving include:

"Is the evidence for lack of control over your craving true 100% of the time?"
"Is there evidence that it might not be true 100% of the time?"
"Do you really drink every time you have a craving and have always done so?"
"Have there been times when you have not experienced craving in a craving-inducing situation?"
"Can you recall one episode when your craving stopped once it had started?"
"Have there been times when you could have given in to your craving and did not?"

Once this is done, the client should write the evidence in the right-hand column of the worksheet under the heading 'Evidence against'. The practitioner should ensure evidence is challenged and re-interpreted sequentially.

Step 4
The client should begin to consider what the evidence suggests. They should be probed to write a brief summary of their conclusions under the heading 'Outcome'. After this is done they should re-rate the strengths of their original beliefs. At this stage the client will have probably realized that some of their uncontrollability beliefs about craving may not be completely grounded in evidence. Despite this, they may still doubt that

they can have some control over their craving. This is because they are likely to have some reservations about the new thought that craving can be controlled. These reservations are natural and are typically expressed in the form of the "yes . . . but" sentences discussed in Chapter 3.

Appendix I   *Decision sheet on past slips*

Decision Sheet on Past Slips					
Preceding event/situation	Apparently irrelevant decision	What could have been done differently?	Advantages of doing things differently	Disadvantages of doing things differently	Safe alternative

Appendix J *Decision sheet on upcoming events*

Decision Sheet on Upcoming Events					
Preceding event/situation	Apparently irrelevant decision	What could be done differently?	Advantages of doing things differently	Disadvantages of doing things differently	Safe alternative

Appendix K *Identifying permissive beliefs*

Identifying Permissive Beliefs		
Activating event	Feelings and sensations	Permissive beliefs
When did it happen? Where were you? What were you doing? What were you thinking about?	What feelings and body sensations did you notice?	What were you saying to yourself that made it easier to keep drinking? Highlight the key belief that makes it most likely for you to continue drinking.

Step 1
The client should note down the activating event of a drinking episode, running through the questions at the bottom of the table under the heading 'Activating event'.

Step 2
Under the heading 'Feelings and sensations', the client should write down the feelings (e.g. anxiety, sadness, worry) and sensations they noticed before the drinking escalated.

Step 3
Under the heading 'Permissive beliefs', the client should write down all the beliefs they had before the drinking got out of control. They should ensure they identify the key belief (the belief that most increases chances of continuing drinking) and highlight it. Clients should be recommended to practise doing this exercise whenever possible over several weeks.

Appendix L *Challenging permissive beliefs*

Challenging Permissive Beliefs

Activating event	Feelings and sensations	Permissive beliefs	Evidence not supporting the beliefs	Alternative beliefs	Strength of alternative beliefs
When did it happen? Where were you? What were you doing? What were you thinking about?	What feelings and body sensations did you notice?	What were you saying to yourself that made it easier to keep drinking? Highlight the key belief that makes it most likely to continue drinking.	Use the questions presented to challenge your belief.	Note the alternative more helpful belief.	Rate the strength of your belief on a scale from 0 to 100%.

Step 1
The client needs to use the information from the previous exercise (activating event, associated feelings and sensations, and permissive beliefs). The key permissive belief should be highlighted.

Step 2
Under the heading 'Evidence not supporting the beliefs', the client should write down all the evidence that suggests that the beliefs are not true. The practitioner can use the following questions during this process:

"Do these beliefs make it easier or harder to drink?"
"What would you say to someone else?"
"What have you learned from drinking in the past that could help you now?"
"Are you being misled by your feelings?"
"What are the consequences of thinking in this way?"
"What could you say to yourself that would make it easier to stop drinking?"
"What would someone else say about this belief?"
"Is this situation similar to past situations?"

Step 3
Under the heading 'Alternative beliefs', the client should record alternative and more balanced beliefs. The above questions for challenging permissive beliefs should be used.

Step 4
Finally, the client should rate the strength of their beliefs to be true on a scale from 0 to 100%.

Appendix M *Identifying positive beliefs*

Identifying Positive Beliefs		
Activating event	Feelings and sensations	Positive beliefs
When did it happen? Where were you? What were you doing? What were you thinking about?	What feelings and body sensations did you notice?	What were you saying to yourself that made it easier to start drinking? Highlight the key belief that makes it most likely for you to start drinking.

Step 1
The client should note down the activating event of a drinking episode, running through the questions at the bottom of the table under the heading 'Activating event'.

Step 2
Under the heading 'Feelings and sensations', the client should write down the feelings (e.g. anxiety, sadness, worry) and sensations they noticed before the drinking escalated.

Step 3
Under the heading 'Positive beliefs', the client should write down all the beliefs they had before the drinking started. They should ensure they identify the key belief (the belief that most increases the chances of starting to drink) and highlight it. Clients should be recommended to practise doing this exercise whenever possible over several weeks.

Challenging positive beliefs

Challenging Positive Beliefs

Activating event	Feelings and sensations	Positive beliefs	Evidence not supporting the beliefs	Alternative beliefs	Strength of alternative beliefs
When did it happen? Where were you? What were you doing? What were you thinking about?	What feelings and body sensations did you notice?	What were you saying to yourself that made it easier to start drinking? Highlight the key belief that makes it most likely to start drinking.	Use the questions presented to challenge your belief.	Note the alternative more helpful belief.	Rate the strength of your belief on a scale from 0 to 100%.

Step 1
The client needs to use the information from the previous exercise (activating event, associated feelings and sensations, and positive beliefs). The key positive belief should be highlighted.

Step 2
Under the heading 'Evidence not supporting the beliefs', the client should write down all the evidence that suggests that the beliefs are not true. The practitioner can use the following questions during this process:

"Do these beliefs make it easier or harder to drink?"
"What would you say to someone else?"
"What have you learned from drinking in the past that could help you now?"
"Are you being misled by your feelings?"
"What are the consequences of thinking in this way?"
"What could you say to yourself that would make it easier to stop drinking?"
"What would someone else say about this belief?"
"Is this situation similar to past situations?"

Step 3
Under the heading 'Alternative beliefs', the client should record alternative and more balanced beliefs. The above questions for challenging permissive beliefs should be used.

Step 4
Finally, the client should rate the strength of their beliefs to be true on a scale from 0 to 100%.

Appendix O *Hierarchy of difficult situations*

Hierarchy of Difficult Situations	
Situation	Difficulty (0–100%)

Step 1
The client can begin by identifying all the situations in which they find it difficult not to drink. These should be listed under the heading 'Situation'.

Step 2
Under the heading 'Difficulty', the client should rate each situation on a scale from 0 to 100%, with 0 being 'not at all difficult' and 100 being 'extremely difficult'. Once they have done this, they should rank the situations in ascending order of difficulty under the heading 'Rank'.

Appendix P *Drinking postponement experiment*

	Drinking Postponement Experiment			
	Before experiment		After experiment	
	Belief to be tested and strength (0–100%)		Belief to be tested and strength (0–100%)	
Experiment to test belief	Possible problems	Strategies to deal with problems	Date of experiment	Experiment outcome

Step 1
The client should start by writing, in their own words, the uncontroll-ability belief they are going to test at the top of the worksheet and then rate its strength before carrying out the experiment.

Step 2
Starting from the easiest situation, the client should write what they plan to do under the heading 'Experiment to test belief'. In order to increase the probability of success, the practitioner should help the client think about possible problems that may arise during the experiment. These should be recorded under the heading 'Possible problems'. After the client has completed this part of the exercise, they should write down how they plan to deal with problems identified (if they do occur) under the heading 'Strategies to deal with problems'.

Step 3
The experiment should be carried out ensuring that the client starts from the easiest situation. Once the experiment is completed, the client should record the outcome under the heading 'Experiment outcome', and re-rate the strength of the original belief. Once this is done, the client should repeat the procedure with the next most difficult situation until they reach the top of the hierarchy.

Appendix Q *Activity diary*

Activity Diary							
Week:	Monday	Tuesday	Wednesday	Thursday	Friday	Saturday	Sunday
9–10	Walking P7/M5						
10–11							
11–12							
12–1							
1–2							
2–3							
3–4							
4–5							
5–6							
6–7							
7–12							

P = Pleasure (from 0 to 10); M = Mastery (from 0 to 10).

Appendix R *Controlled drinking skills*

Controlled Drinking Skills	
Before drinking	Whilst drinking

Appendix S   *Controlled drinking programme*

Controlled Drinking Programme		
Key targets	What to remember	Strategic plan

| Appendix T | *Plan for managing high-risk situations*

Plan for Managing High-Risk Situations	
Situation	Response

References

American Psychiatric Association (1994). *Diagnostic and Statistical Manual of Mental Disorders (DSM-IV).*Washington, DC: American Psychiatric Association.

Babor, T. F., de la Fuente, J. R., Saunders, J., & Grant, M. (1992). *The Alcohol Use Disorders Identification Test: Guidelines for Use in Primary Healthcare.* Geneva: World Health Organization.

Babor, T. F., del Boca, F. K., & McRee, B. (1997). Estimating measurement error in alcohol dependence symptomatology: findings from a multisite study. *Drug & Alcohol Dependence, 45*, 13–20.

Bandura, A. (1977). *Social Learning Theory.* Englewood Cliffs, NJ: Prentice Hall.

Beck, A. T. (1976). *Cognitive Therapy and the Emotional Disorders.* New York: New American Library.

Beck, A. T. (2005). The current state of cognitive therapy: a 40-year retrospective. *Archives of General Psychiatry, 62*, 953–959.

Beck, A. T., Brown, G., Epstein, N., & Steer, R. A. (1988). An inventory for measuring clinical anxiety: Psychometric properties. *Journal of Consulting and Clinical Psychology, 56*, 893–897.

Beck, A. T., Emery, G., & Greenberg, R. L. (1985). *Anxiety Disorders and Phobias: a Cognitive Perspective.* New York. Basic Books.

Beck, A.T., Ward, C. H., Mendelson, M., Mock, J., & Erbaugh, J. (1961). An inventory for measuring depression. *Archives of General Psychiatry, 4*, 561–571.

Beck, A. T., Wright, F. D., Newman, C. F., & Liese, B. S. (1993). *Cognitive Therapy of Substance Abuse.* New York: Guildford Press.

Beck, J. (1995). *Cognitive Therapy: Basics and Beyond.* New York: The Guilford Press.

Benson, H. (1975). *The Relaxation Response.* New York: William Morrow.

Blackburn, I. M., James, I. A., Milne, D. L., Baker, C., Standart, S., Garland, A., & Reichelt, K. (2001). The Revised Cognitive Therapy Scale: Psychometric properties. *Behavioural and Cognitive Psychotherapy, 29*, 431–446.

Broe, S. (1995). D+E+S+C=how to deal with difficult people. *Early Childhood News, 7*, 34–36.

Brown, S. A., Christiansen, B. A., & Goldman, M. S. (1987). Alcohol Expectancy Questionnaire: An instrument for the assessment of adolescent and adult alcohol expectancies. *Journal of Studies on Alcohol, 48*, 483–491.

Brown, S. A., Goldman, M. S., Inn, A., & Anderson, L. R. (1980). Expectations of reinforcement from alcohol: their domain and relation to drinking patterns. *Journal of Consulting and Clinical Psychology, 48*, 419–426.

Bruch, M. H., & Bond, F. W. (Eds.) (1998). *Beyond Diagnosis: Case Formulation Approaches in CBT.* Chichester: Wiley.

Cahalan, D., Cisin, I. H., & Crossley, H. M. (1969). American drinking practices: a national study of drinking behavior and attitudes. *Rutgers Center of Alcohol Studies, Monograph No. 6.* New Brunswick, NJ.

Carroll, K. M. (1998). *A Cognitive-Behavioral Approach: Treating Cocaine Addiction*. Rockville, MD: National Institute on Drug Abuse.

Christiansen, B. A., Smith, G. T., Roehling, P. V., & Goldman, M. S. (1989). Using alcohol expectancies to predict adolescent drinking behaviour after one year. *Journal of Consulting and Clinical Psychology, 57,* 93–99.

Cone, J. D. (1997). Issues in functional analysis in behavioral assessment. *Behaviour Research and Therapy, 35,* 259–275.

Conigrave, K. M., Degenhardt, L. J., Whitfield, J. B., Saunders, J. B., Helander, A., & Tabakoff, B. (2002). CDT, GGT, and AST as markers of alcohol use: The WHO/ISBRA collaborative project. *Alcoholism: Clinical and Experimental Research, 26,* 332–339.

Cooper, M. L. (1994). Motivations for alcohol use among adolescents: Development and validation of a four-factor model. *Psychological Assessment, 6,* 117–128.

Cooper, M. L. (1995). Drinking to regulate positive and negative emotions. *Journal of Personality and Social Psychology, 69,* 990–1005.

Copello, A., Orford, J., Hodgson, R., & Tober, G. (2009). *Social Behaviour and Network Therapy for Alcohol Problems*. London: Routledge.

Cox, W. M., & Klinger, E. (1988). A motivational model of alcohol use. *Journal of Abnormal Psychology, 97,* 168–180.

Darkes, J., & Goldman, M. S. (1993). Expectancy challenge and drinking reduction: Experimental evidence for a mediational process. *Journal of Consulting and Clinical Psychology, 61,* 334–353.

Dattilo, F. M. (2002). Homework assignments in couple and family therapy. *Journal of Clinical Psychology, 58,* 535–547.

Derogatis, C. R. (1977). *Administration, Scoring, and Procedures Manual for the (Revised) Version and Other Instruments of the Psychopathology Rating Scales Series*. New Haven, CT: Johns Hopkins University School of Medicine.

D'Zurilla, T. J., & Goldfried, M. R. (1971). Problem-solving and behavior modification. *Journal of Abnormal Psychology, 78,* 107–126.

Ellis, A. (1975). *A New Guide to Rational Living*. North Hollywood: Wilshire Book Company.

Fals-Stewart, W., O'Farrell, T. J., Birchler, G. R., Cordova, J., & Kelley, M. L. (2005). Behavioral couples therapy for alcoholism and drug abuse: Where we've been, where we're going. *Journal of Cognitive Psychotherapy, 19,* 229–246.

Fernie, B. A., & Spada, M. M. (2008). Metacognitions about procrastination: A preliminary investigation. *Behavioural and Cognitive Psychotherapy, 36,* 359–364.

Fernie, B. A., Spada, M. M., Nikčević, A. V., Georgiou, G., & Moneta, G. B. (2009). Metacognitive beliefs about procrastination: Development and concurrent validity of a self-report questionnaire. *Journal of Cognitive Psychotherapy, 23,* 283–293.

Folstein, M. F., Folstein, S. E., & McHugh, P. R. (1975). Mini-mental state. A practical method for grading the cognitive state of patients for the clinician. *Journal of Psychiatry Research, 12,* 189–198.

Gessel, A. H. (1989). Edmund Jacobson, MD, PhD: The founder of scientific relaxation. *International Journal of Psychosomatics, 36,* 1–4.

Glasser, W. (1985). *Positive Addiction*. New York: Harper Collins.

Goldfried, M. R., & Sprafkin, R. (1976). *Behavioral Personality Assessment*. Morristown, NJ: General Learning Press.

Goldman, M. S., del Boca, F. K., & Darkes, J. (1999). Alcohol expectancy theory: The application of cognitive neuroscience. In H. Blane & K. Leonard (Eds.), *Psychological Theories of Drinking and Alcoholism* (pp. 203–246). New York: Guilford Press.

Gorman, D. M. (2001). Developmental processes. In N. Heather, T. J. Peters, & T. Stockwell (Eds.), *International Handbook of Alcohol Dependence and Problems* (pp. 339–356). Chichester: John Wiley & Sons.

Hawton, K., Salkovskis, P., Kirk, J., & Clark, M. (1989). *Cognitive Behaviour Therapy for Psychiatric Problems: A Practical Guide.* Oxford: Oxford University Press.

Heather, N., & Robertson, I. (1983). Controlled Drinking. London: Methuen.

Heaton, S. K., Chelune, G. J., Talley, J. L., Kay, G. G., & Curtiss, G. (1993). *Wisconsin Card Sorting Test Manual: Revised and Expanded.* Odessa, FL: Psychological Assessment Resources.

Helzer, J. E., & Pryzbeck, T. R. (1988). The co-occurrence of alcoholism with other psychiatric disorders in the general population and its impact on treatment. *Journal of Studies on Alcohol, 49,* 219–224.

Higgins, S. T., Silverman, K., & Heil, S. H. (2003). Behavioral interventions for problem drinking: Community reinforcement and contingency management. In B. Johnson, P. Ruiz, & M. J. Galanter (Eds.), *Handbook of Clinical Alcoholism Treatment* (pp. 111–118). Baltimore, MD: Lippincott, Williams & Wilkins.

Horn, J. L., Wanberg, K. H., & Foster, F. M. (1990). *Guide to the Alcohol Use Inventory (AUI).* Minneapolis, MN: National Computer Systems.

Howard, M. O., Elkins, R. L., Rimmele, C., & Smith, J. W. (1991). Chemical aversion treatment of alcohol dependence. *Drug and Alcohol Dependence, 29,* 107–143.

Inskip, H. M., Harris, E. C., & Barraclough, B. (1998). Lifetime risk of suicide for affective disorder, alcoholism and schizophrenia. *British Journal of Psychiatry, 172,* 35–37.

Kabat-Zinn, J., Lipworth, L., & Burney, R. (1985). The clinical use of mindfulness meditation for the self-regulation of chronic pain. *Journal of Behavioral Medicine, 8,* 163–190.

Kolb, D. A. (1984). *Experiential Learning: Experience as the Source of Learning and Development.* Englewood Cliffs, NJ: Prentice-Hall.

Kushner, M. G., Sher, K. J., & Beitman, B. D. (1990). The relation between alcohol problems and anxiety disorders. *American Journal of Psychiatry, 147,* 685–695.

Lambert, M. J., & Ogles, B. M. (2004). The efficacy and effectiveness of psychotherapy. In: M. J. Lambert (Ed.), *Bergin and Garfield's Handbook of Psychotherapy and Behavior Change* (pp. 139–193). New York: Wiley.

Lazar, S. W., Bush, G., Gollub, R. L., Fricchione, G. L., Khalsa, G., & Benson, H. (2000). Functional brain mapping of the relaxation response and meditation. *NeuroReport, 11,* 1581–1585.

Leigh, B. C., & Stacy, A.W. (1993). Alcohol outcome expectancies: Scale construction and predictive utility in higher order confirmatory models. *Psychological Assessment, 5,* 216–229.

Lewis, K. M. (2005). The supervision of cognitive and behavioural psychotherapists. *BABCP Magazine* Supplement, May issue. Accrington, UK: BABCP.

Lightfoot, L. O., & Hodgins, D. (1988). A survey of alcohol and drug problems in incarcerated offenders. *The International Journal of the Addictions, 23,* 687–706.

Linehan, M. (1993). *Cognitive-Behavioral Treatment for Borderline Personality Disorder.* New York: Guilford Press.

Litman, G. K., Stapleton, J., Oppenheim, A. N., & Peleg, M. (1983). An instrument for measuring coping behaviours in hospitalized alcoholics: Implications for relapse prevention treatment. *British Journal of Addiction, 78,* 269–276.

Ludwig, A. M., & Wikler, A. (1974). 'Craving' and relapse to drink. *Quarterly Journal of Studies on Alcoholism, 35,* 108–130.

Marlatt, G. A., & Gordon, J. R. (1985). *Relapse Prevention: Maintenance Strategies in the Treatment of Addictive Behaviors.* New York: Guilford Press.

Mayfield, D., McLeod, G., & Hall, P. (1974). The CAGE questionnaire: Validation of a new alcoholism screening instrument. *American Journal of Psychiatry, 131,* 1121–1123.

Mason, P. (1989). *Managing Drink.* Birmingham: Aquarius.

Mazur, J. (2002). *Learning and Behavior.* New York: Prentice Hall.

McLellan, A. T., Kushner, H., Metzger, D., Peters, R., Smith, L., Grissom, G., Pettinati, H., & Argerious, M. (1992). *Addiction Severity Index.* Philadelphia, PA: Veterans Administration and National Institute on Drugs and Alcohol.

McNally, A. M., & Palfai, T. P. (2001). Negative emotional expectancies and readiness to change among college student binge drinkers. *Addictive Behaviors, 26,* 721–734.

Meier, P., Barrowclough, C., & Donmall, M. (2005). The role of the therapeutic alliance in the treatment of drug abuse. *Addiction, 100,* 500–511.

Miller, B. N., Miller, M. N., Verhegge, R., Linville, H. H., & Pumariega, A. J. (2002). Alcohol use among college athletes: Self medication for psychiatric symptoms? *Journal of Drug Education, 32,* 41–52.

Miller, P. M. (1975). A behavioural intervention program for chronic problem drunkenness offenders. *Archives of General Psychiatry, 32,* 915–918.

Miller, W. R. (1983). Motivational interviewing with problem drinkers. *Behavioural Psychotherapy, 11,* 147–172.

Miller, W. R., & Marlatt, G. A. (1984). *Manual for the Comprehensive Drinker Profile.* Odessa, FL: Psychological Assessment Resources.

Miller, W. R., & Rollnick, S. (2002). *Motivational Interviewing: Preparing People for Change* (2nd Ed.). New York: Guilford Press.

Miller, W. R., & Tonigan, J. S. (1996). Assessing drinkers' motivation for change: The Stages of Change Readiness and Treatment Eagerness Scale (SOCRATES). *Psychology of Addictive Behaviors, 10,* 81–89.

Miller, W. R., Wilbourne, P. L., & Hettema, J. E. (2003). What works? A summary of alcohol treatment outcome research. In R. K. Hester, & W. R. Miller (Eds.), *Handbook of Alcoholism Treatment Approaches: Effective Alternatives* (pp. 13–63). Boston, MA: Allyn & Bacon.

Monti, P. M., Kadden, R., Rohsenow, D. J., Cooney, N., & Abrams, D. (2002). *Treating Alcohol Dependence: A Coping Skills Training Guide* (2nd Ed.). New York: Guilford Press.

Monti, P. M., Rohsenow, D. J., Colby, S. M., & Abrams, D. B. (1995). Coping and social skills training. In R. K. Hester, & W. R. Miller (Eds.), *Handbook of Alcoholism Treatment Approaches: Effective Alternatives* (pp. 221–241). Needham Heights, MA: Allyn & Bacon.

Moos, R. H. (1990). Conceptual and empirical approaches to developing family-based assessment procedures: Resolving the case of the Family Environment Scale. *Family Process, 29,* 199–208.

Moos, R. H., Fenn, C. B., Billings, A. G., & Moos, B. S. (1988). Assessing life stressors and social resources: Applications to alcoholic patients. *Journal of Substance Abuse, 1,* 135–152.

Moscicki, E. K. (1997). Identification of suicide risk factors using epidemiologic studies. *Psychiatric Clinics of North America, 20,* 499–517.

Niaura, R. S., Rohsenow, D. J., Binkoff, J. A., Monti, P. M., Pedraza, M., & Abrams, D. B.

(1988). Relevance of cue reactivity to understanding alcohol and smoking relapse. *Journal of Abnormal Psychology, 97,* 133–152.

O'Brien, C. P., Childress, A. R., McClellan, T., & Ehrman, R. (1990). Integrating systemic cue exposure with standard treatment in recovering drug dependent patients. *Addictive Behaviors, 15,* 355–365.

Papageorgiou, C., & Wells, A. (2000). Treatment of recurrent major depression with attention training. *Cognitive and Behavioral Practice, 7,* 407–413.

Papageorgiou, C., & Wells, A. (2001). Metacognitive beliefs about rumination in recurrent major depression. *Cognitive and Behavioral Practice, 8,* 160–164.

Papageorgiou, C., & Wells, A. (2003). An empirical test of a clinical metacognitive model of rumination and depression. *Cognitive Therapy and Research, 27,* 261–273.

Prien, R. F., Himmelhoch, J. M., & Jupfer, D. J. (1988). Treatment of mixed mania. *Journal of Affective Disorders, 182,* 9–15.

Prochaska, J. O., & DiClemente, C. C. (1986). Toward a comprehensive model of change. In W. R. Miller, & N. Heather (Eds.), *Treating Addictive Behaviors: Processes of Change* (pp. 3–27). New York: Plenum Press.

Raistrick, D., Heather, N., & Godfrey, C. (2006). *Review of the Effectiveness of Treatment for Alcohol Problems.* London: National Treatment Agency for Substance Misuse.

Rimmele, C. T., Howard, M. O., & Hilfrink, M. L. (1995). Aversion therapies. In: R. K. Hester, & W. R. Miller (Eds.), *Handbook of Alcoholism Treatment Approaches: Effective Alternatives* (pp. 134–147). Boston, MA: Allyn & Bacon.

Rogers, Carl (1961). *On Becoming a Person: A Therapist's View of Psychotherapy.* London: Constable.

Rohsenow, D. J., Niaura, R. S., Childress, A. R., Abrams, D. B., & Monti, P. M. (1991). Cue reactivity in addictive behaviors: Theoretical and treatment implications. *International Journal of the Addictions, 25,* 957–993.

Rosenthal, R. N., & Westreich, L. (1999). Treatments of persons with dual diagnoses of substance use disorder and other psychological problems. In B. S. McCrady, & E. E. Epstein (Eds.), *Addictions: A Comprehensive Guidebook* (pp. 439–476). New York: Open University Press.

Russell, M., Martier, S. S., Sokol, R. J., Mudar, P., Bottoms, S., Jacobson, S., & Jacobson, J. (1994). Screening for pregnancy risk-drinking. *Alcoholism: Clinical and Experimental Research, 18,* 1156–1161.

Siegel, S. (1983). Classical conditioning, drug tolerance, and drug dependence. In R. G. Smart, F. B. Glasser, Y. Israel, H. Kalant, R. E. Popham, & W. Schmidt (Eds.), *Research Advances in Alcohol and Drug Problems,* Vol. 7 (pp. 207–246). New York: Plenum.

Skinner, B. F. (1969). *Contingencies of Reinforcement.* Englewood Cliffs, NJ: Prentice-Hall.

Skinner, H. A., & Allen, B. A. (1982). Alcohol dependence syndrome: Measurement and validation. *Journal of Abnormal Psychology, 91,* 199–209.

Smith, J. E., & Meyers, R. J. (1995). The community reinforcement approach. In R. Hester, & W. Miller (Eds.), *Handbook of Alcoholism Treatment Approaches: Effective Alternatives* (pp. 251–266). New York: Allyn & Bacon.

Sobell, L. C., Brown, J., Leo, G. I., & Sobell, M. B. (1996). The reliability of the Alcohol Timeline Followback when administered by telephone and by computer. *Drug and Alcohol Dependence, 42,* 49–54.

Sobell, M. B., & Sobell, L. C. (1993). *Problem Drinkers: Guided Self-Change Treatment.* New York: Guilford Press.

Spada, M. M. (2006a). Cognitive-behavioural case formulation in the treatment of alcohol problems. In A. V. Nikčevič, A. Kuczmierczyk, & M. H. Bruch (Eds.), *Formulation and Treatment in Clinical Health Psychology* (pp. 19–41). London: Brunner-Routledge.

Spada, M. M. (2006b). *Overcoming Problem Drinking: A Self-help Guide Using Cognitive Behavioural Strategies*. Colchester: Constable Robinson.

Spada, M. M., Caselli, G., & Wells, A. (2009). Metacognitions as a predictor of drinking status and level of alcohol use following CBT in problem drinkers: A prospective study. *Behaviour Research and Therapy, 47*, 882–886.

Spada, M. M., & Wells, A. (2005). Metacognitions, emotion and alcohol use. *Clinical Psychology and Psychotherapy, 12*, 150–155.

Spada, M. M., & Wells, A. (2006). Metacognitions about alcohol use in problem drinkers. *Clinical Psychology and Psychotherapy, 13*, 138–143.

Spada, M. M., & Wells, A. (2008). Metacognitive beliefs about alcohol use: development and validation of two self-report scales. *Addictive Behaviors, 33*, 515–527.

Spada, M. M., & Wells, A. (2009). A metacognitive model of problem drinking. *Clinical Psychology and Psychotherapy, 16*, 383–393.

Spada, M. M., Zandvoort, M., & Wells, A. (2007). Metacognitions in problem drinkers. *Cognitive Therapy and Research, 31*, 709–716.

Spanier, G. (1976). Measuring dyadic adjustment: New scales of assessing the quality of marriage and similar dyads. *Journal of Marriage and the Family, 38*, 15–28.

Spanier, G. (1979). The measurement of marital quality. *Journal of Sex and Marital Therapy, 5*, 288–300.

Spielberger, C. D., Russell, G. J., & Crane, R. S. (1983). Assessment of anger: The State-Trait Anger Scale. In J. N. Butcher, & C. D. Spielberger (Eds.), *Advances in Personality Assessment* (pp. 159–187). Hillsdale, NJ: LEA.

Stacy, A. W., Widaman, K. F., & Marlatt, G. A. (1990). Expectancy models of alcohol use. *Journal of Personality and Social Psychology, 58*, 918–928.

Stewart, J., Dewit, H., & Eikelboom, R. (1984). Role of unconditioned and conditioned drug effects in the self-administration of opiates and stimulants. *Psychological Review, 91*, 251–268.

Sullivan, J. T., Sykora, K., Schneiderman, J., Naranjo, C. A., & Sellers, E. M. (1989). Assessment of alcohol withdrawal: The revised Clinical Institute Withdrawal Assessment for alcohol scale (CIWA-Ar). *British Journal of Addiction, 84*, 1353–1357.

Thorley, A. (1980). Medical response to problem drinking. *Medicine, 35*, 1816–1827.

Timmerman, I. G. H., & Emmelkamp, P. M. G. (2006). The relationship between attachment styles and Cluster B personality disorders in prisoners and forensic inpatients. *International Journal of Law and Psychiatry, 29*, 48–56.

Tolman, E. C. (1932). *Purposive Behavior in Animals and Men*. New York: Appleton-Century-Crofts.

Velleman, R. (1992). *Counselling for Alcohol Problems*. London: Sage.

Wanberg, K. W., Horn, J. L., & Foster, F. M. (1977). A differential assessment model for alcoholism: The scales of the Alcohol Use Inventory. *Journal of Studies on Alcohol, 38*, 512–543.

Ward, M. (1988). *Helping Problem Drinkers – A Practical Guide for the Caring Professions*. Canterbury: Kent Council for Addictions.

Wechsler, D. (1997). *WAIS-III Administration and Scoring Manual*. San Antonio, TX: The Psychological Corporation.

Weiss, R. D., Najavits, L. M., & Greenfield, S. F. (1999). A relapse prevention group for patients with bipolar and substance use disorders. *Journal of Substance Abuse Treatment*, *16*, 47–54.

Wells, A. (1997). *Cognitive Therapy of Anxiety Disorders*. Chichester: Wiley.

Wells, A. (2000). *Emotional Disorders and Metacognition: Innovative Cognitive Therapy*. Chichester: Wiley.

Wilson, G. T. (1988). Alcohol and anxiety. *Behavioural Research and Therapy*, *26*, 369–381.

Witkiewitz, K., Marlatt, G. A., & Walker, D. D. (2005). Mindfulness-based relapse prevention for alcohol and substance use disorders. *Journal of Cognitive Psychotherapy*, *19*, 211–228.

Ziedonis, D. M., Smelson, D., Rosenthal, R. N., Batki, S., Green, A. I., Henry, R. J., Montoya, I., Parks, J., & Weiss, R. D. (2005). Improving the care of individuals with schizophrenia and substance use disorders: consensus recommendations. *Journal of Psychiatric Practice*, *11*, 315–339.

Zywiak, W. H., Connors, G. J., Maisto, S. A., & Westerberg, V. S. (1996). Relapse research and the Reasons for Drinking Questionnaire: A factor analysis of Marlatt's relapse taxonomy. *Addiction*, *91*, S121–S130.

Index

The abbreviation CBT is used for cognitive behaviour therapy. Page references in *italic* indicate Figures and Tables, which can also be found listed in full after the Contents.